For all IT Men !

Table of Contents

The Story behind the *Succinctly* Series of Books 7

    Information is plentiful but harder to digest 7

    The *Succinctly* series 7

    The best authors, the best content 7

    Free forever 8

    Free? What is the catch? 8

    Let us know what you think 8

About the Author 9

    A special thanks 9

Chapter 1 What is BizTalk Server? 10

    BizTalk Server Architecture 10

    Who is This Book For? 11

Chapter 2 Getting Started with BizTalk Server 12

    Installing BizTalk Developer Edition 12

        Installing BizTalk 13

        Configuring BizTalk Server 14

Chapter 3 Developer Environment 17

    Introduction 17

    Available Developer Artifacts 18

    Explaining the Developer Artifacts 19

Chapter 4 How All the Artifacts Work Together 21

Chapter 5 Schemas 23

Manage Schema Nodes	24
Properties for Schema Nodes	26
Schemas File Properties	28
Schemas Operations inside Visual Studio	30
Generate Schema from XML file	32
Property Promotion	34

Chapter 6 Mappings 37

Introduction	37
Mapper Overview	37
Adding a Map to the Project	38
Add the Schemas to the Map	39
Link Nodes	40
Functoids	43
Available Functoids	46
Maps Operations inside Visual Studio	53
Test Map	53
Validate Map	55
Debug Map	58

Chapter 7 Pipelines 60

Introduction	60
Custom Pipelines	63

Chapter 8 Orchestrations 65

Introduction	65
Toolbox	66
Orchestration Designer	66
Orchestration Overview	66

    Available Shapes 66

    Creating a Simple Orchestration 68

Chapter 9 Deploy to the Server using Visual Studio **83**

    Deployment 83

Chapter 10 Configuring the BizTalk Administrator **87**

    One Last Note 97

Staying on the cutting edge

About the Author

Rui Machado is a developer and software engineer. Born in Portugal, he has a strong .NET background and a special interest in scripting languages. He has a bachelor's degree in information technologies and a post-graduate degree in business intelligence. He is currently finishing his master's degree in informatics. He works for ALERT Life Sciences Computing, a Portuguese Software House for Healthcare Solutions as a Software Developer and Engineer in the Business Intelligence Department. He works in the business intelligence department of ALERT Life Sciences Computing, a Portuguese software house for healthcare solutions.

Rui is a technology enthusiast with a lot of love for programming languages. Although most of his time is spent working for and with technology, he also manages to have time for other activities like skateboarding, surfing, and enjoying life with friends and family.

A special thanks

Many people throughout my career have helped me become the professional that I am today—people who allowed me to develop my passion for technology and gave me their knowledge because they believed I could put it to good use. My coworker Sandro Pereira is one of those people. He taught me that sharing knowledge with others is a gain for all our community members and everyone who works for the evolution of technology. Thank you to all my family and friends who keep believing in me and what I work for.

Chapter 1 What is BizTalk Server?

In a very simplistic way, BizTalk Server can be considered a message router or broker. For example, when an external system sends an EDI (Electronic Data Interchange) message, BizTalk will be able to easily read the message and convert it to the message type that the destination system expects.

To make an analogy with the real world scenario, you can consider BizTalk as a logistics platform for exchange merchandise. The raw materials come into the company and are stored, processed, transformed, and sent to customers. And likewise, electronic messages are received, validated, stored, processed, and sent to other systems.

BizTalk includes a messaging infrastructure, dehydration and rehydration functionalities, more than 25 multi-platform adapters, a rules engine (BRE), the ability to obtain performance information on critical business processes, debug, persistence, and treatment and error-recovery transactions. BizTalk Server is the main Microsoft integration platform, ideal for use with Enterprise Application Integration (EAI), Business to Business (B2B) integration, and Business Process Management (BPM) solutions.

BizTalk is an integration solution that requires considerable investments that might not be affordable for small and middle enterprises. However, it can be worthwhile when your company starts saving some money. Microsoft has a nice case study on this: AMC Entertainment, by using this integration platform, is now saving more than 2.6 million dollars a year, and it recouped its investment in the solution in about six months for a 200 percent annual return on investment. This case study shows you how this process-oriented technology can help you save money. AMC justified its cost with reduced payments to vendors because it uses the solution to buy its supplies through a 153,000-item online catalog with wholesale and discounted rates, rather than continuing to purchase supplies independently from local suppliers. I recommend that you read the entire case study.

BizTalk Server Architecture

The BizTalk Server runtime is built on a publish–subscribe architecture in which a message is published into the system, and then received by one or more active subscribers. All messages are received by BizTalk through physical ports, called Receive Ports. A Receive Port is a logical container for one or several Receive Locations. The Receive Locations are where you specify the details about the transport to be used, the exact address where the message is to be received, and any other specific properties to that transport type, as you can see in Figure 1:

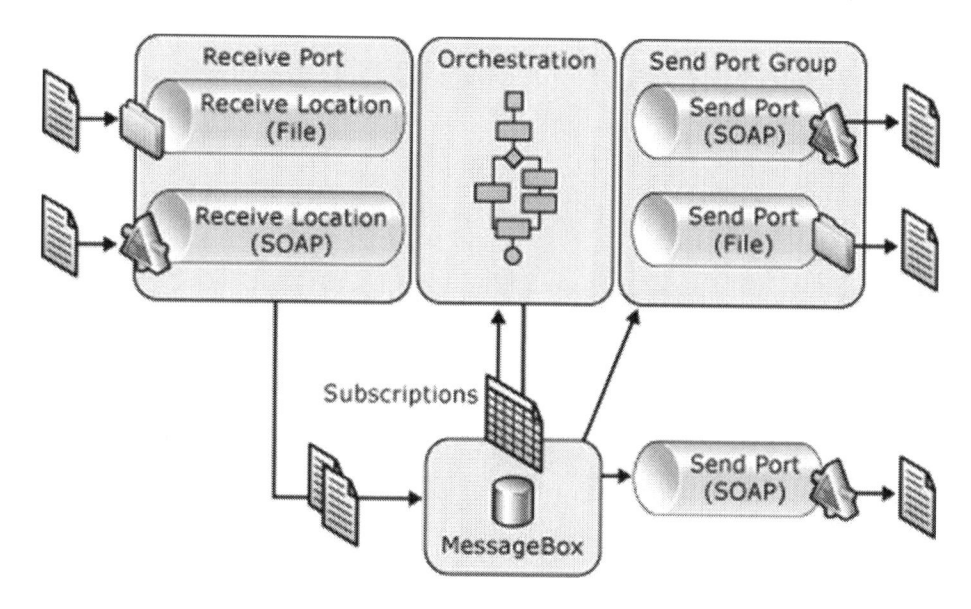

Figure 1: BizTalk Server Messaging Architecture

There are two core concepts behind the BizTalk Server architecture that you should be aware of:

- The MessageBox Database
- Single sign-on (SSO) mechanism

The MessageBox is the heart of the publish–subscribe engine in BizTalk Server. It is made of two components: an SQL Database and the Message Agent. The SQL Database is used to persist all metadata and data surrounding an application such as messages, message properties, subscriptions, orchestration states, tracking data, and host queues for routing. The Message Agent provides a layer of abstraction over the message box database. It uses the .NET COM interop to expose a set of APIs that the BizTalk Core engine can use to communicate with the message box database (publishing messages, subscribing to messages, retrieving messages, and so on).

Single sign-on is a mechanism that provides a way to map a Windows user ID to non-Windows user credentials; this simplifies the way BizTalk can access diverse systems connected to it and how these diverse systems connect to BizTalk Server.

Who is This Book For?

This book is written primarily for BizTalk developers, .NET developers, and all those who are passionate about systems integration. Although integration and BPM consultants mainly use BizTalk, I want to show .NET developers how can they use this platform as another option for their careers.

Chapter 2 Getting Started with BizTalk Server

Installing BizTalk Developer Edition

System Requirements

So that you can start practicing everything you will be learning from this e-book, you can install a free Developer Edition of BizTalk Server (to date, it's only available for free in BizTalk Server 2010) provided by Microsoft. We will be using BizTalk Server 2010, even though BizTalk Server 2013 R2 has already been launched. The 2010 version is still one of the most-used versions, and there are many more resources related to this version, so if you are starting in this platform it is easier to find tutorials, videos, and examples than for it 2013 or 2013 R2.

You can find the software here or you can download the evaluation VM here.

To install it, make sure you meet all of the following hardware and software requirements.

To be run BizTalk Server 2010 you need:

- 32-bit (x86) platforms: Computer with an Intel Pentium-compatible CPU that is 1 GHz or faster for single processors, 900 MHz or faster for double processors, or 700 MHz or faster for quad processors.
- 64-bit (x64) platforms: Computer with a CPU that is compatible with the AMD64 and Extended Memory 64-bit Technology (EMT64T), 1.7 GHz or faster processor recommended for BizTalk Server 2010.
- 2 GB of RAM minimum (more is recommended).
- 10 GB of available hard-disk space.
- VGA monitor (1024 x 768) or higher-resolution monitor.

To use and develop for BizTalk Server 2010 you need the following software:

- Microsoft Windows: Can be Windows 7, Windows Server 2008 R2, Windows Server 2008 SP2, or Windows Vista® with Service Pack 2 (SP2).
- SQL Server 2008 R2 or SQL Server 2008 SP1
- Microsoft .NET Framework 4 and .NET Framework 3.5 with Service Pack 1 (SP1)
- Microsoft Visual Studio 2010 (Required for selected features only)
- Microsoft Office Excel 2010 or 2007 (Required for selected features only)
- SQL Server 2005 Notification Service (Required for selected features only)

- SQLXML 4.0 with Service Pack 1 (Required for selected features only)
- Internet Information Services (IIS) Version 7.5 and 7.0 (Required for selected features only)

> *Note: BizTalk is an enterprise product and should be installed in a Server Operating System like Windows Server.*

These requirements come as-is from Microsoft's webpage; however, I suggest you install Visual Studio—otherwise you won't be able to develop BizTalk projects.

Installation

Assuming that all machines are already installed with the operating system with the latest critical Windows updates from Microsoft and all other prerequisites are met, let's start the installation of BizTalk Server 2010 free edition.

In this e-book I will assist you in a basic installation so that you can try the examples you will be seeing in the following chapters on your own. Although it might look simple, you should be aware that this is a platform that will have access to multiple data sources in multiple companies, so if you want to install BizTalk in a production environment, I advise you to study it more thoroughly.

Installing BizTalk

As you start the setup you will be presented with a welcome page with several options. Please select **Install Microsoft BizTalk Server 2010** to initialize a basic installation.

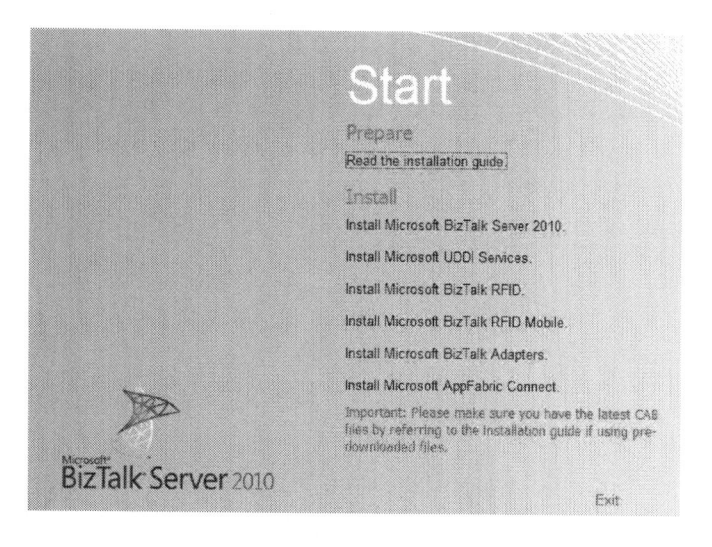

Figure 2: Installing BizTalk Server

After selecting the option to install Microsoft BizTalk Server 2010, you will be prompted with several configuration options. For this installation, you can leave the default options. Just make sure that the **Developer Tools and SDK** option is selected, as it is the feature that allows us to develop mapping and orchestrations in Visual Studio.

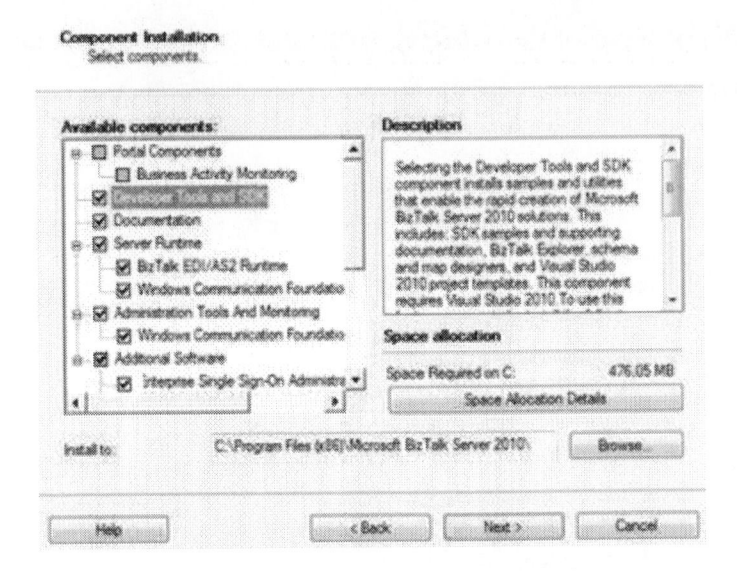

Figure 3: Selecting the Tools and SDK option

Configuring BizTalk Server

When the setup completes you will be prompted with the configurations screen for BizTalk Server 2010; this is where you configure your database connection and your credentials for accessing the database where BizTalk Server will store all your application's metadata.

The first screen lets you choose between basic and custom configuration, and as you see in the option description, you should choose the **Basic** configuration. You also need to configure your database server name, which in my case is **ADMIN-PC**, and the Service credential to access this database server, as shown in Figure 4:

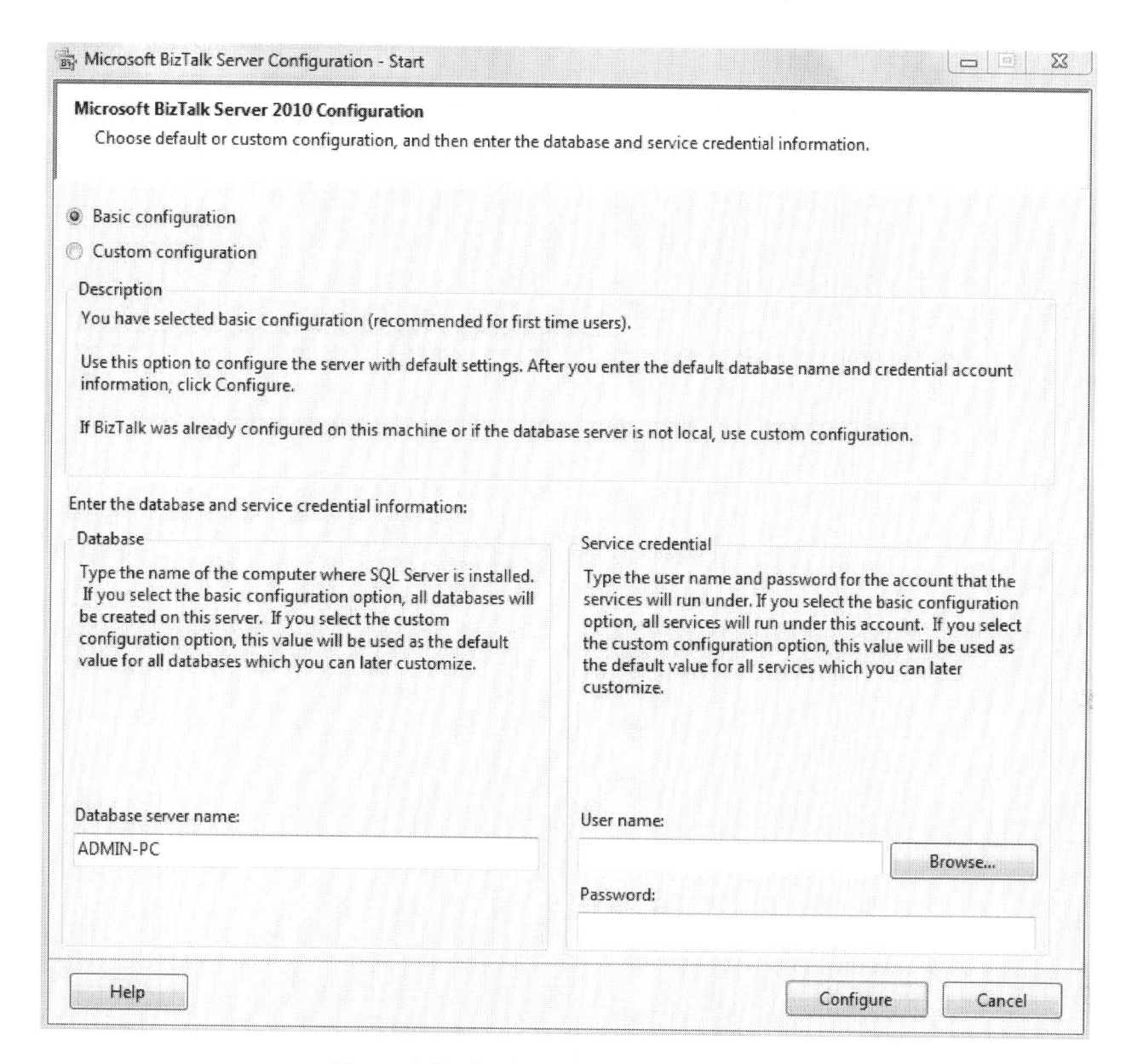

Figure 4: Configuring BizTalk Server 2010

After you configure your database server connections, click on the **Configure** option and the setup will make the connections and configurations for you, as you can see in the following figure:

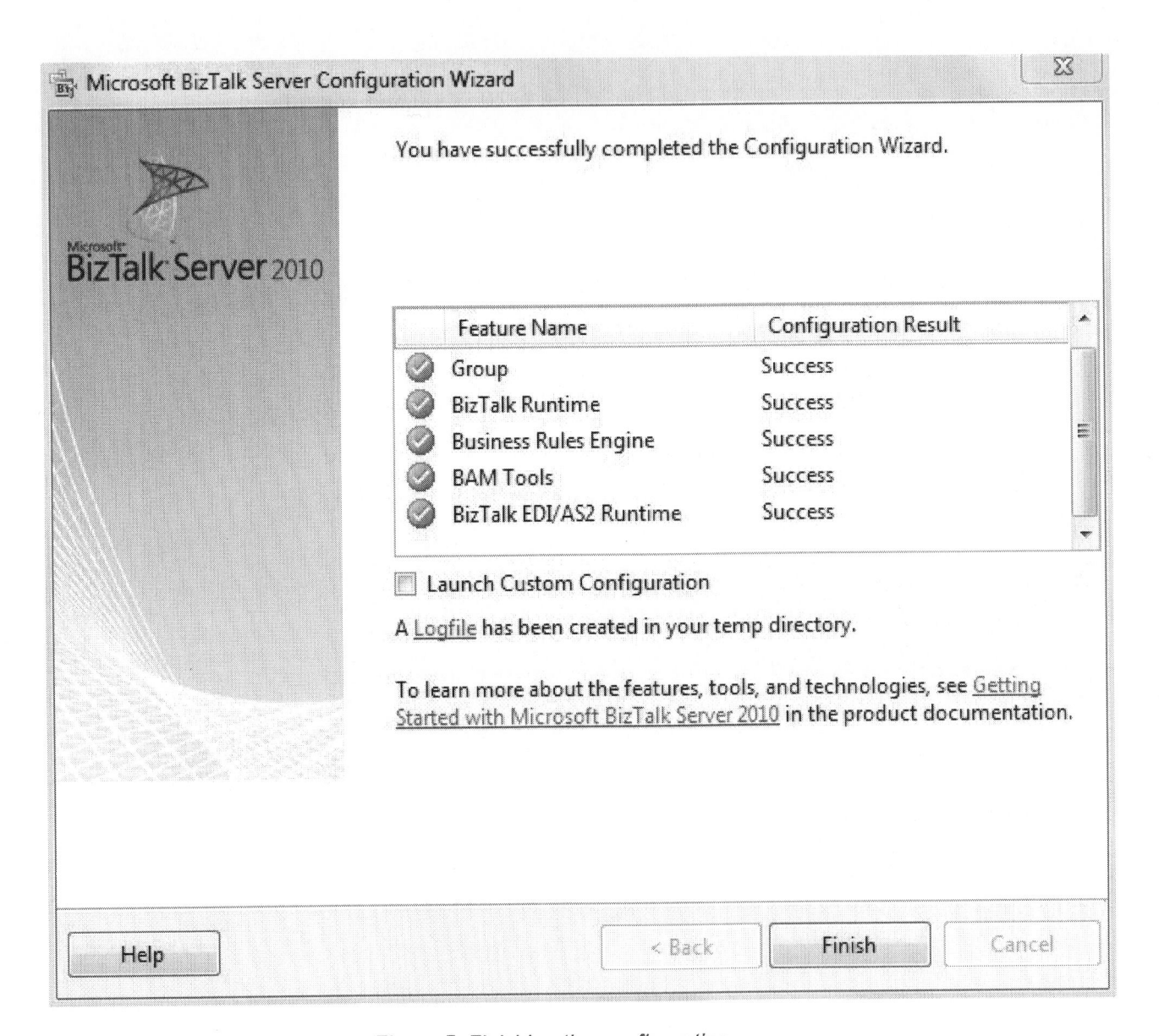

Figure 5: Finishing the configuration

At the end of the configuration, a LogFile is created in your temp directory. Any time an error occurs, you can look inside this file for further information about the problem.

Chapter 3 Developer Environment

Introduction

As you can see, Visual Studio is your main developer tool, allowing you to create applications to be further deployed and installed in BizTalk Server platform. The first time you start a new Empty BizTalk Server Project, you might be a little bit lost, because you will be presented with an empty page with no options in the toolbox. That's because Visual Studio will show you different tools and options depending on which BizTalk artifact you want to create.

After you finish all the configuration items, you are ready to start developing in BizTalk Server 2010. Open Visual Studio and start a new BizTalk Server Project (Empty BizTalk Server Project).

Figure 6: Creating a new project

Available Developer Artifacts

To check the full list of artifacts, right-click the project in the Solution Explorer and click **Add > New Item**. This will prompt a new screen with the following options:

- BizTalk Orchestration
- Map
- Receive Pipeline
- Send Pipeline
- Flat File Schema
- Property Schema
- Schema
- Flat File Schema Wizard

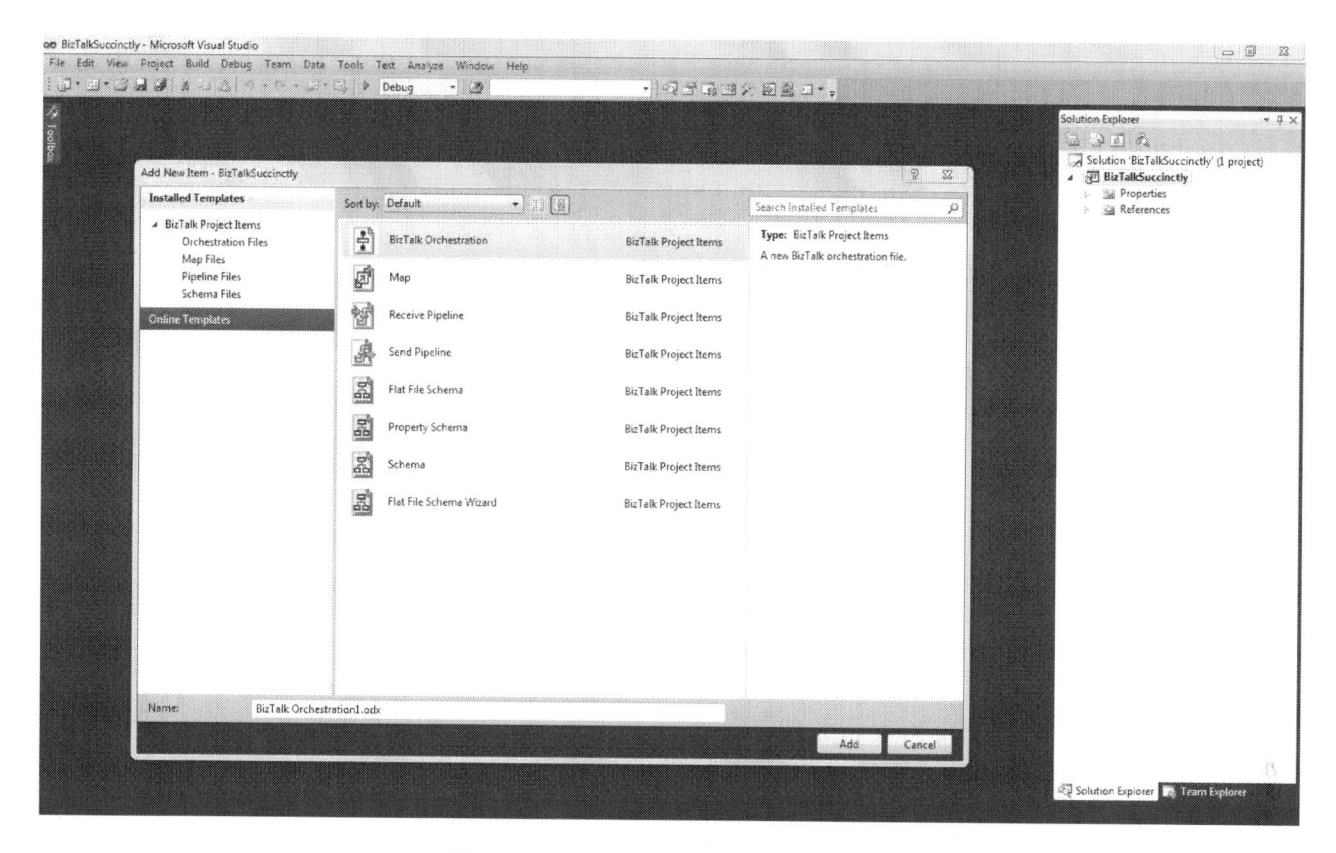

Figure 7: Development artifacts

Explaining the Developer Artifacts

You will see the Add New Item screen very often during your development, as you will need several items to accomplish a final solution. I will be talking in further detail about each of these items in the following chapters, but here is a brief overview:

Table 1: BizTalk Server project artifacts

Item	Description
Map	Maps are graphical representations of Extensible Stylesheet Language Transformation (XSLT) documents that allow us to perform, in a simple and visual manner, transformations between XML messages
Receive Pipeline	A pipeline that is executed on messages after they have been received by an adapter and before they are published into the MessageBox database.
Send Pipeline	A pipeline that is executed on messages before they are sent out of the BizTalk Server; they are responsible for making the message "End System-ready".

Item	Description
Flat File Schema	Defines the structure of a flat file schema with all the necessary information in the form of annotations in a XML Schema.
Property Schema	A property schema is a BizTalk-specific schema that defines field elements to be exposed to the BizTalk messaging engine. The property schema is associated with a message schema from which the values will be promoted into the message context. These properties can be accessed by the messaging engine for use in routing, correlation, and tracking
Schema	This is an abstraction of an XML file, specifying its nodes, data type, and namespace. Defines the skeleton of a XML file, such as a class for the skeleton of an object in object-oriented programming. A schema might also be viewed as an agreement on a common vocabulary for a particular application that involves exchanging documents. Microsoft BizTalk Server uses the XML Schema Definition (XSD) language to define the structure of all messages that it processes, and refers to these definitions of message structure as schemas. With few exceptions, structured messages are the core of any application.
Orchestration	An orchestration is the visual executable implementation of a business process flow, that is, a logical and chronological set of activities in order to achieve a goal.

We will now explore each of these development items so that by the time you finish this book you can start developing your own application integration solutions using Microsoft BizTalk Server 2010.

Chapter 4 How All the Artifacts Work Together

The BizTalk Server is a product developed by Microsoft as a response to the increasing variety of disparate systems and the need to exchange messages between them.

The need for this kind of tool is easy to understand as computer-based Information Systems have their own data structures, document structures, and workflows, and exchanging documents between companies or just separate systems demands an alignment between the business processes. We need to integrate these so that when a message arrives, it is fully integrated with the workflow it is meant to trigger.

This kind of alignment requires middleware tools that can capture the messages that need to be exchanged, apply all transformations and business rules required by the target, and make sure that the message is integrated in the correct business process in its systems. BizTalk Server fits in this middleware platform and its main role is to respond to this need of business process integration.

While working with systems integration there are several challenges that need to be fulfilled and understood, including the format and structure of the documents. When the middleware platform captures a message, it doesn't know its structure, which nodes it contains, or the destination system. But there are plenty more potential problems, such as if the document structure meets the destination's expected structure and the workflow it needs to follow.

All of these problems and many more are resolved by developing BizTalk Server applications with the use of several objects that you can develop and combine. In this book we will take a tour of each set of artifacts, which are:

- Schemas
- Ports
- Pipelines
- Maps
- Orchestrations

In addition to the BizTalk Server applications artifacts, there are several more artifacts, such as adapters, that are basically software components that enable you to easily send messages out of or receive messages into BizTalk Server with a delivery mechanism that conforms to a commonly recognized standard. They will be explained in more detail throughout the book. Figure 8 provides an overview of how all these artifacts work together within a BizTalk Server application.

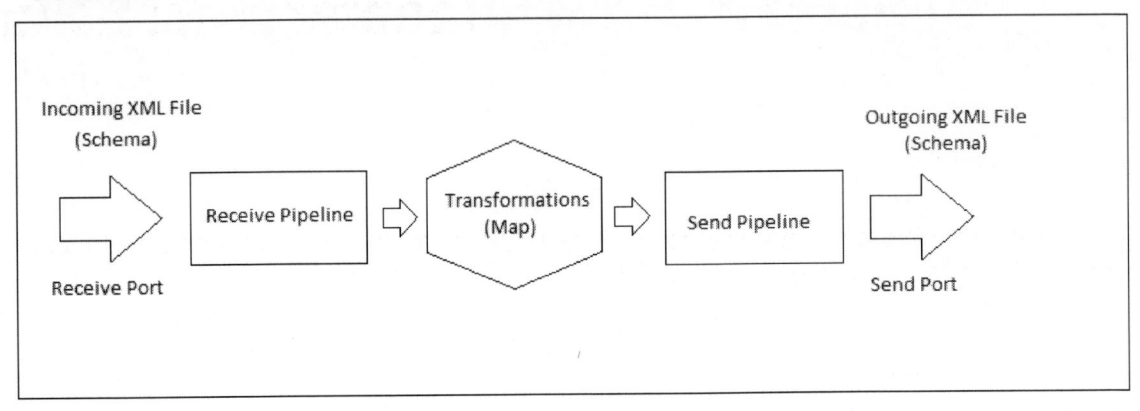

Figure 8: Simple Applications

Chapter 5 Schemas

Introduction

A schema is a file that defines the hierarchical structure of a XML file, much as a class defines an object in object-oriented programming. These files, which have the XML Schema Definitions (XSD) extension, must have a root node and any another elements and attributes as you wish. After an XSD is defined for an application, BizTalk will use it to validate any XML file that comes in through a receive port, and if it matches, that XML will be transformed and sent to any subscriber of that XSD format.

Schemas are the core basic artifacts of BizTalk because they describe and identify the type of the messages that BizTalk will process, and you must be aware that normally BizTalk only process messages that it knows. They are referenced by other artifacts like orchestrations and maps.

BizTalk Server supports the following four types of schemas:

1. **XML schema**. An XML schema defines the structure of a class of XML instance messages. Because this type of schema uses XSD language to define the structure of an XML instance message. This is the intended purpose of XSD, as such schemas use XSD in a straightforward way.

2. **Flat file schema**. A flat file schema defines the structure of a class of instance messages that use a flat file format, either delimited or positional, or some combination thereof. Because the native semantic capabilities of XSD do not accommodate all of the requirements for defining the structure of flat file instance messages—such as the various types of delimiters that might be used for different records and fields within the flat file—BizTalk Server uses the annotation capabilities of XSD to store this extra information within an XSD schema. BizTalk Server defines a rich set of specific annotation tags that can be used to store all of the required additional information.

3. **Envelope schema**. An envelope schema is a special type of XML schema. Envelope schemas are used to define the structure of XML envelopes, which are used to wrap one or more XML business documents into a single XML instance message. When you define an XML schema to be an envelope schema, a couple of additional property settings are required, depending on such factors as whether there are more than one root record defined in the envelope schema.

4. **Property schema**. A property schema is used with one of the two mechanisms that exist within BizTalk Server for what is known as property promotion. Property promotion is the process of copying specific values from deep within an instance message to the message context. From the message context, these values are more easily accessed by various BizTalk Server components. These components use the values to perform actions such as message routing. Promoted property values can also be copied in the other direction, from the more easily accessible message context back into the depths of the instance message, just before the instance message is sent to its destination. A property schema is a simple version of a BizTalk schema that plays a role in the process of copying promoted properties back and forth between the instance message and the message context.

Besides XML files, BizTalk also uses schemas to describe flat files and any other formats. To add new schemas to your project, select the **Schema** option in Visual Studio, click **Add**, and select **New Item**.

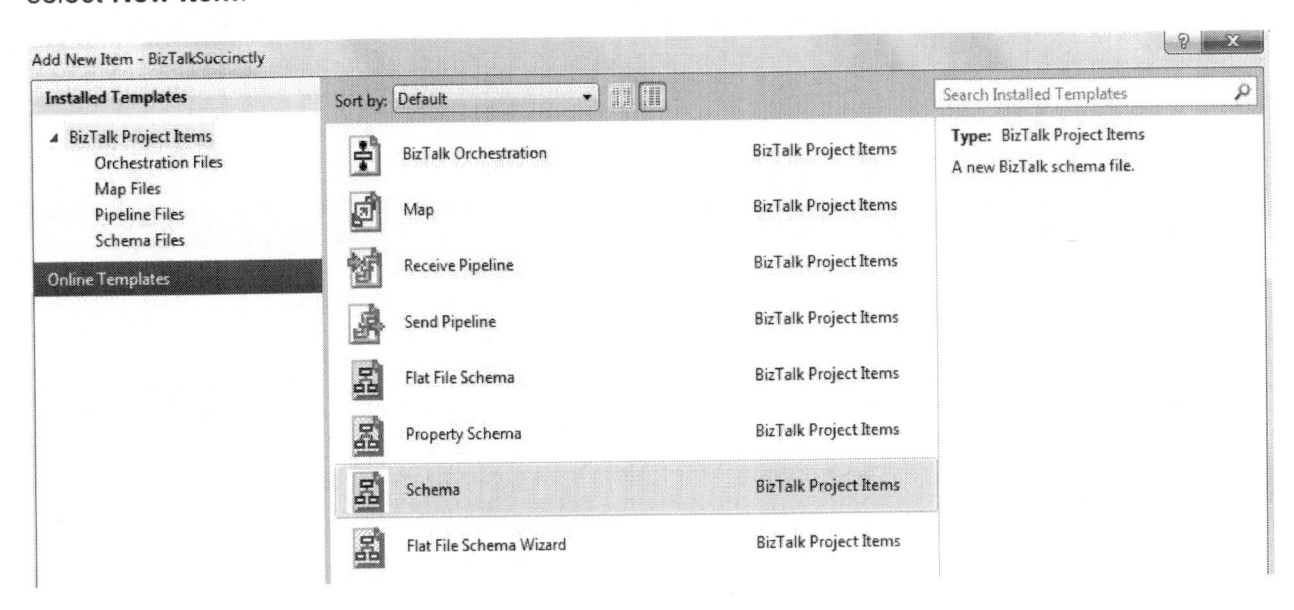

Figure 9: Add new Schema

BizTalk uses a combination of *namespace#rootnode* to define the schema type of a message, thereby making a MessageType unique (for example: http://mynamespace.com#MyRootNode). In other words, BizTalk uses this combination to identify and resolve schema references.

Manage Schema Nodes

After adding a new schema to the project, Visual Studio will open a configuration screen for Schemas in which you can define the nodes, records, and attributes for that XSD file. An important note is that you should always change the root name of the schema, so that BizTalk can properly identify it.

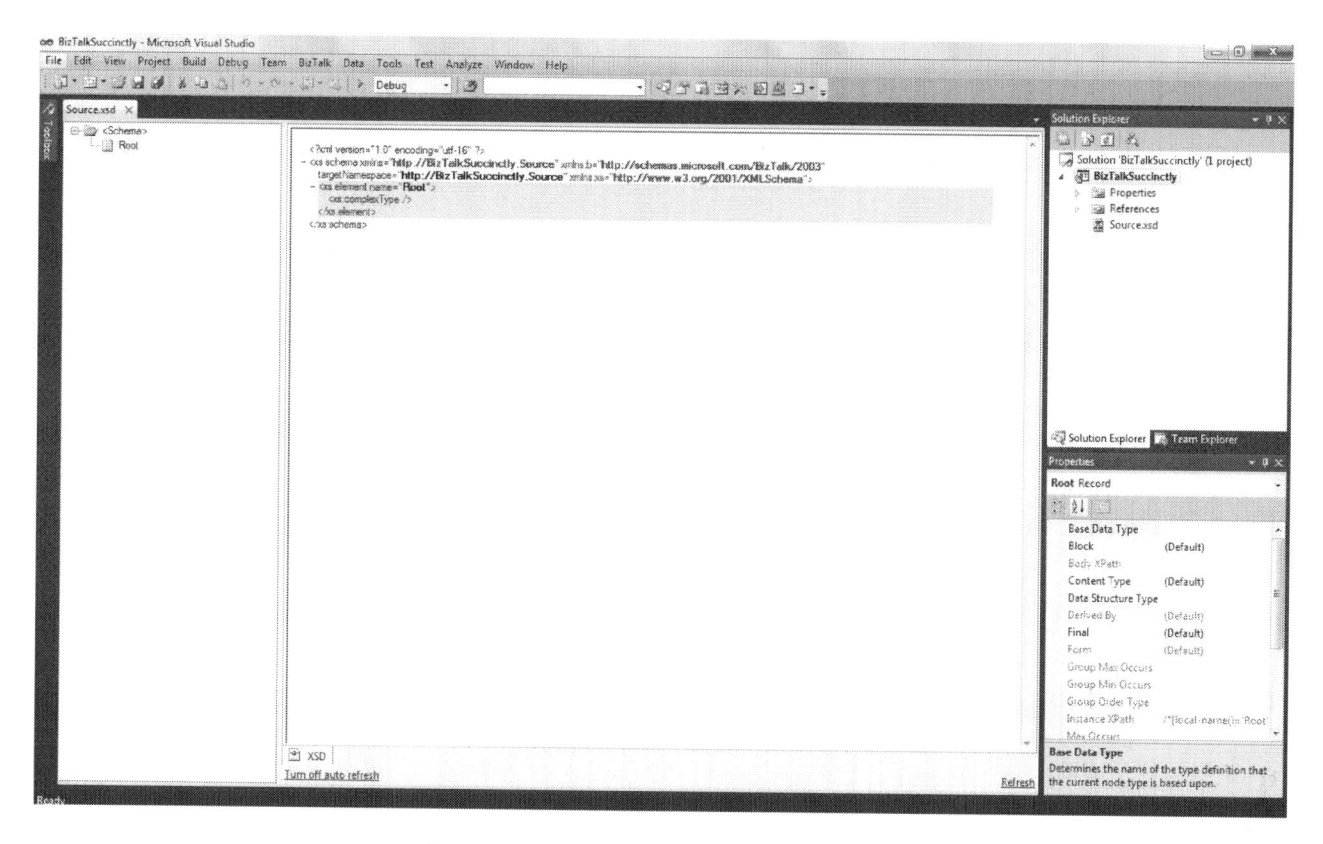

Figure 10: Schema creator screen

In this Visual Studio screen, you can add items (nodes) to your schema. To do so, right-click on the root node on the left side of the screen and select the correct option for your requirements.

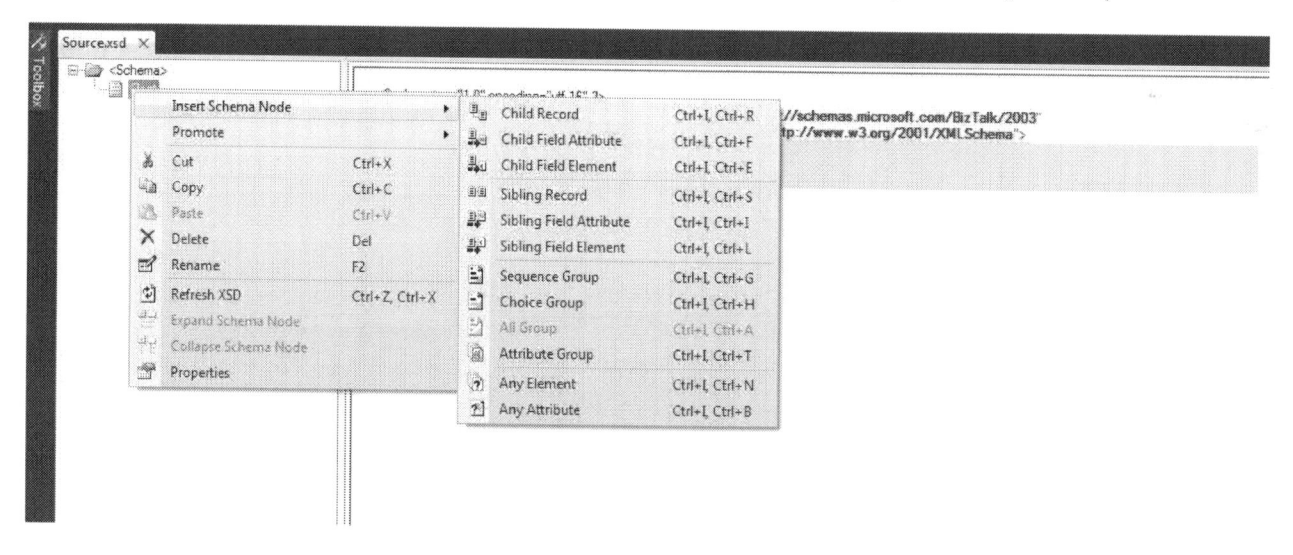

Figure 11: Add nodes to a schema

For this schema I will create basic employee information with name, address, country, telephone number, date of birth, and salary. The resulting schema will appear as shown in Figure 12:

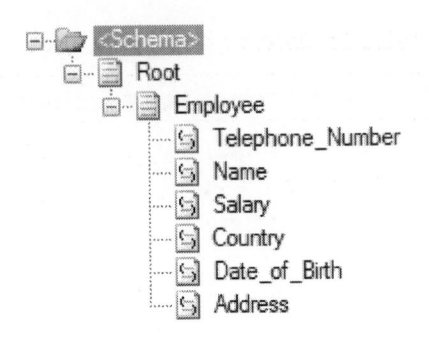

Figure 12: Schema for employee

Properties for Schema Nodes

Although this schema has all the nodes needed to represent our employee, BizTalk allows you to enrich your schema with more definitions, like data type, or which fields are mandatory. This way you can select a node (field elements or attributes) and use the Properties window to define all your node settings. Figure 13 shows you all the available properties after selecting a schema node.

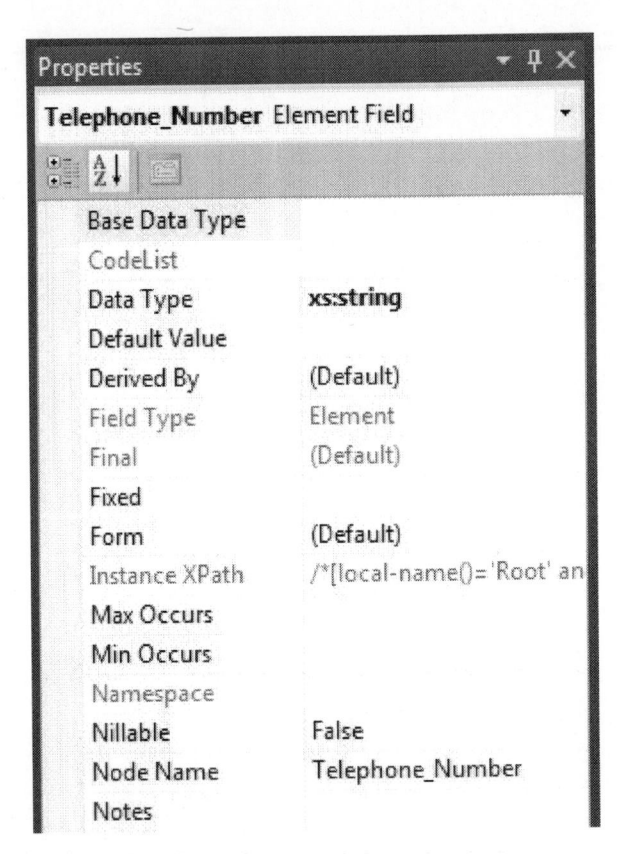

Figure 13: Schema node properties window

Table 2 describes the schema node properties in more detail:

Table 2: Schema Node Properties

Property	Description
Base Data Type	Determines the name of the type definition that the current node type is based upon. Use the **Base Data Type** property to specify the base data type value from which the data type of the selected Record, Field Element, or Field Attribute node will be derived (for example, "xs:string").
Code List	Specifies the reference number for the code list to use with the selected **Field Element** or **Field Attribute** node, and provides access to the **CodeList** dialog box.
Data Type	The data type of the node. (The main types are Decimal, DateTime, String, Int, and Boolean, but BizTalk offers many more options.) Specifies a simple data type for the selected Field Element or Field Attribute node; for example, string, int, Boolean and so on.
Default Value	Specifies the default value for the selected **Field Element** or **Field Attribute** node (like 0 for a quantity).
Derived By	Indicates how the underlying Simple Type of the Field is derived from its base data type.
Field Type	Identifies the selected node as a **Field Element** node or a **Field Attribute** node.
Final	Specifies derivation restrictions for the data type defined for the selected **Record**, **Field Element**, or **Field Attribute** node.
Fixed	Specifies a fixed value for the element(s) or attribute in an instance message that corresponds to the selected **Field Element** or **Field Attribute** node, if the data is present.
Instance XPath	Shows you the Xpath code to access the node in the XML file.
Max/Min Occurs	Number of maximum and minimum occurances of the node
Namespace	Namespace of the node
Nillable	Indicates if the value can be null (Default is False).
Node Name	Name of the node
Notes	Any notes regarding the node

Schemas File Properties

After you manage the settings related to the **Record**, **Field Element**, or **Field Attribute**, BizTalk also lets you define properties for the schema itself, properties that should be always checked as they define how the schema will be identified by the BizTalk engine. To access these properties, just click on your schema file in the Solution Explorer.

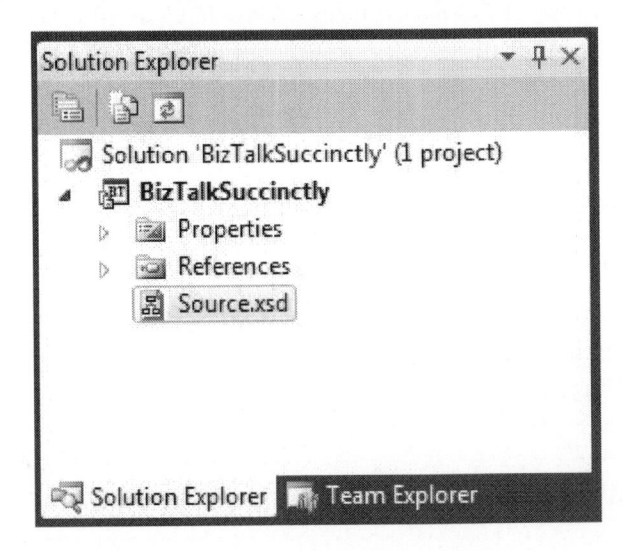

Figure 14: Properties for Schemas

After you select the schema you want to set up, Visual Studio will then display its properties in the Properties window.

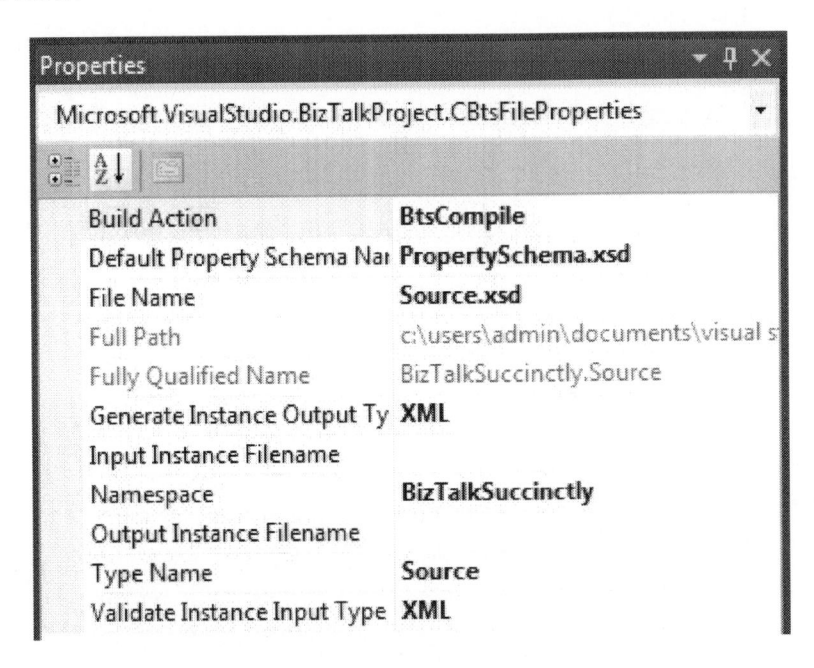

Figure 15: Properties for Schemas definition

All the properties for your schemas are listed and explained in Table 3.

Table 3: Schema Properties

Property	Description
Build Action	Specifies how the file will be processed in the application Build action. (You can specify that a schema will not compile when building a project.)
Default Property Schema Name	Specifies the name of the file generated for promoted properties
File Name	Name of the schema file. You can use this property to examine and set the name of the selected schema file.
Full Path	Location of the schema file. You can use the **Full Path** property to examine the file system location in which the selected schema file is stored.
Fully Qualified Name	This is a concatenation of the namespace and the type name. Together they form the fully qualified name used to uniquely identify a type in .NET framework. You must make sure that no two types in your entire BizTalk environment have the same fully qualified name, because they are used to identify incoming and outcoming messages and which messages are for which subscribers.
Generate instance Output Type	Specify the output type for the generate instance option.
Input Instance Filename	Input the file name for instance validation when using the validate instance input type.
Namespace	The .NET namespace the compiled schema will belong to.
Output Instance FileName	The file name for the generate instance option.
Type Name	.NET type for the compiled schema.
Validate instance Input Type	Specify the output type for the validate instance option.

Schemas Operations inside Visual Studio

Validate Schema

BizTalk offers several options to evaluate the consistency of your schemas, telling you if they are well constructed or if there are errors. To do so, use the Validate Schema option, available when you right-click your schema file in the Solution Explorer and select **Validate Schema**.

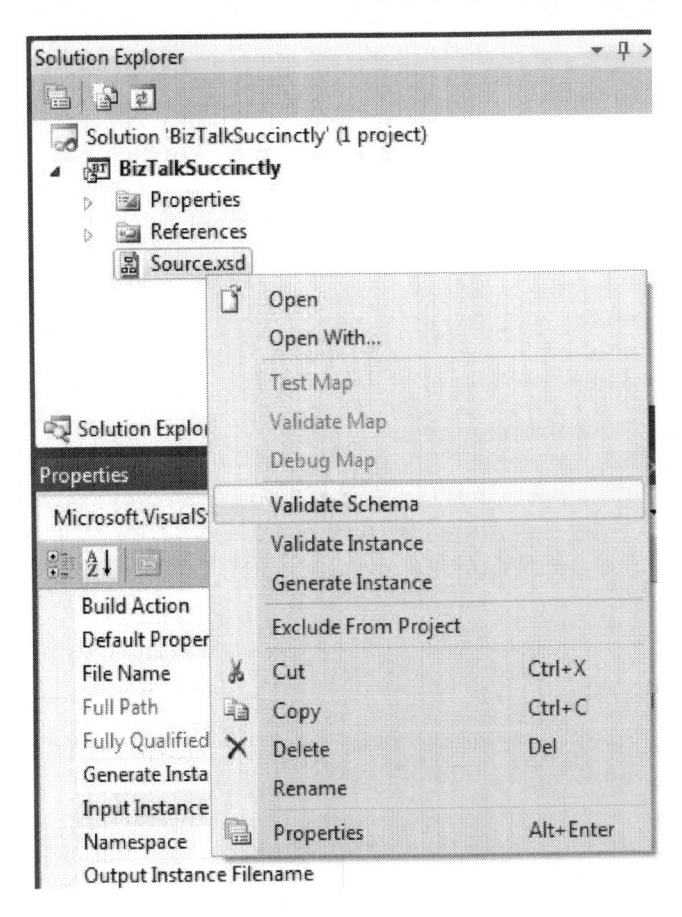

Figure 16: Validate Schemas

BizTalk will return a message mentioning if the schema is well defined or not. BizTalk will also return the file name, so that you can use it for further evaluation. As shown in Figure 17, the schema had no errors:

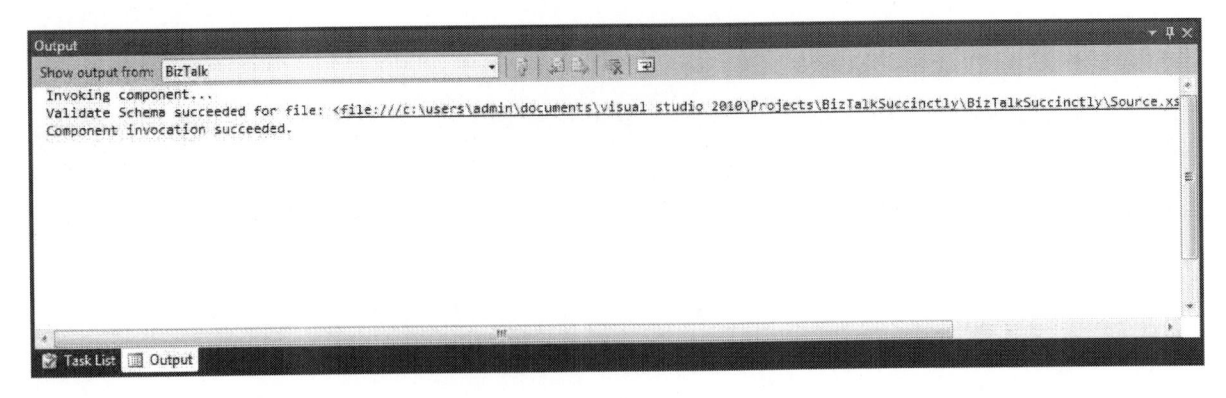

Figure 17: Output window for validate schema

Generate Instance

The Generate Instance feature is used to generate an instance of an XML file or native type for Flat file according to your schema previously created and validated. Although this option also validates the schema, it's a common best practice to validate the schema and then generate the instance. This option is available in the same menu as the Validate Schema option.

Once you click on the **Generate Instance** option, BizTalk will generate an example XML file, with the file name defined in the Output Instance Filename property of the schema with the Generate Instance Output Type. Figure 18 shows a XML instance for our employee schema.

```
- <ns0:Root xmlns:ns0="http://BizTalkSuccinctly.Source">
   - <Employee>
       <Telephone_Number>Telephone_Number_0</Telephone_Number>
       <Name>Name_0</Name>
       <Salary>Salary_0</Salary>
       <Country>Country_0</Country>
       <Date_of_Birth>Date_of_Birth_0</Date_of_Birth>
       <Address>Address_0</Address>
     </Employee>
  </ns0:Root>
```

Figure 18: Generate instance for employee schema

This generated instance can now be used as an example to evaluate our schema using the Validate Instance option.

Validate Instance

The Validate Instance feature allows you to validate if an XML file or native type for Flat file has the structure of a schema file, and so, is of that format. This option is available in the same menu as the Validate Schema menu.

To use this option, you need to change the schema property Input Instance Filename, defining the XML file name (full path) so that the schema uses the XML file you want to validate when using this Validate Instance option. After changing the property and running the validator, BizTalk will show you the result in the output window. As you can see in Figure 19, BizTalk validated our XML file with success.

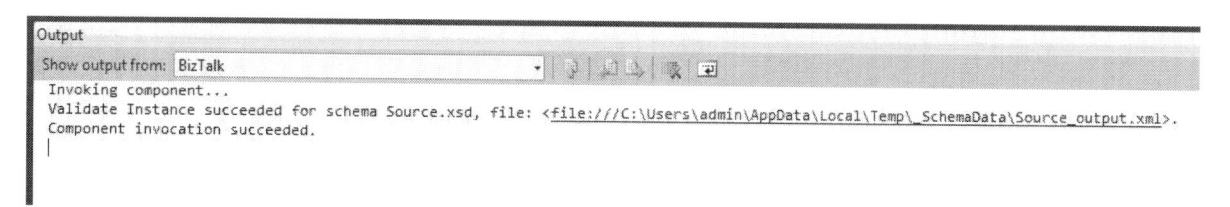

```
Output
Show output from: BizTalk
Invoking component...
Validate Instance succeeded for schema Source.xsd, file: <file:///C:\Users\admin\AppData\Local\Temp\_SchemaData\Source_output.xml>.
Component invocation succeeded.
```

Figure 19: Validate Instance

Generate Schema from XML file

One nice feature of BizTalk is the capability of generating XSD files from an XML instance. This is important for BizTalk developers, as it allows them to ask their clients for a single XML example of the files being integrated, and then generate a schema to use in their maps. (This approach has some limitations and may require you to manually set some properties or elements.)

To use this option, right-click your project in the Solution Explorer panel and then select **Add**, **Add Generated Items**, and then select the option **Generate Schema** as shown in Figure 20.

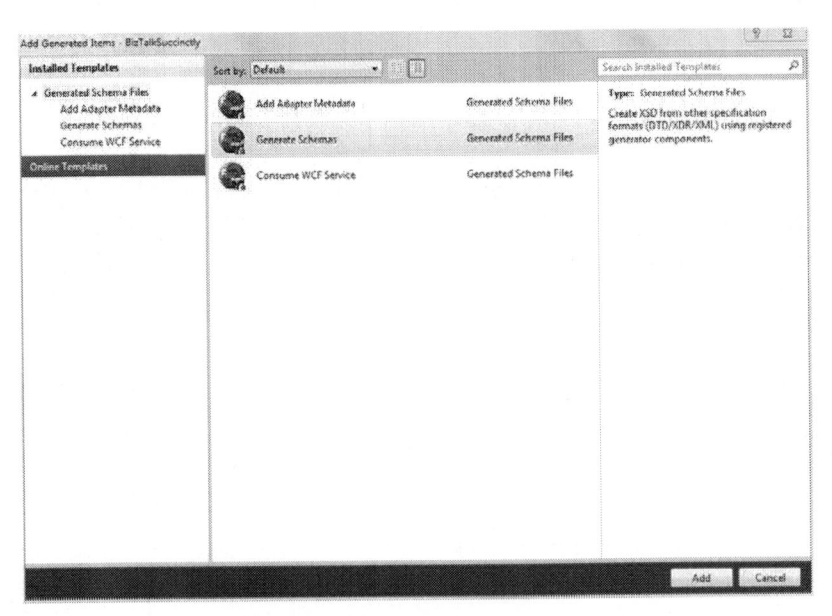

Figure 20: Generate Schemas

After the Generate Schema screen appears, you need to select the document format. As you are using our employee XML, we need to select **Well-Formatted XML** and specify the XML file path.

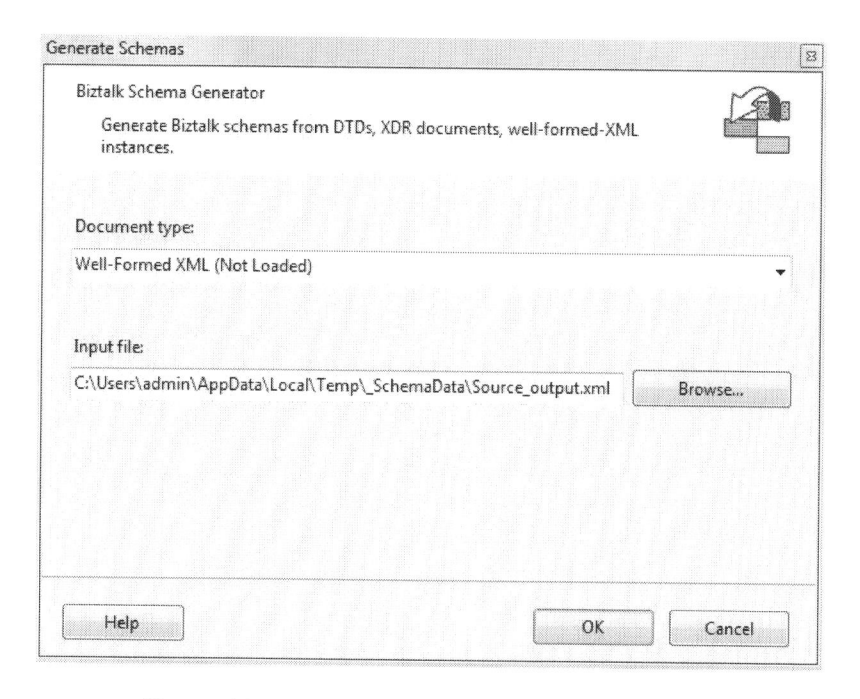

Figure 21: Generate Schema Specifications

When you finish specifying the document type and the input file path, click **OK**, and BizTalk will generate the XSD file. If you get an error indicating that the module isn't loaded, you need to execute the module installer on the path shown in the message box (you might need to execute it using the CMD with elevated privileges). After that, you're ready to go.

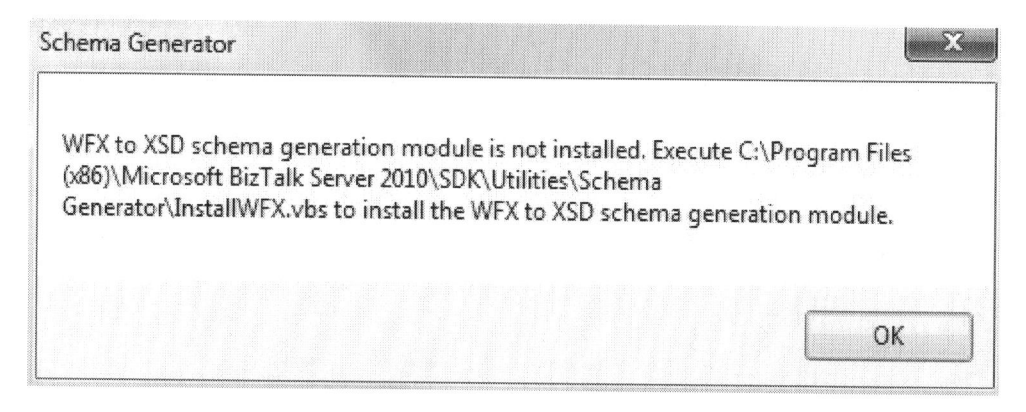

Figure 22: Generate Schema error

By the end of the generation, you will be able to see your brand new schema in the Solution Explorer window. In our case the name is Source_output.xsd:

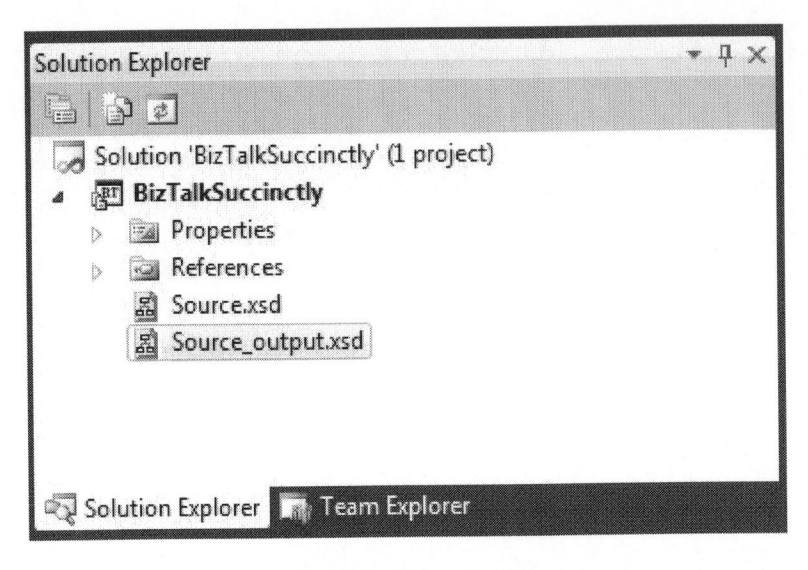

Figure 23: New Generated Schema

Property Promotion

BizTalk provides two types of property promotions: distinguished fields and property fields.

In a simplified manner, distinguished fields can only be used within orchestration, while promoted property fields can be accessed through all phases of the BizTalk message processing, either in orchestrations or from custom code, routing, and pipelines.

Distinguished Fields

BizTalk Server has mechanisms that allow you to use elements in schemas to do routing or logical operations based on the values the XML instances have in those elements. The first mechanisms I want to talk about are distinguished fields.

These distinguished fields are fields from a message that have been marked as distinguished using this feature in the BizTalk schema editor. These fields, when marked as distinguished, can then be used through dot notation in orchestrations and can be used to both access the value from this specific field and to set the value of this field. They differ from promoted properties, as they are not written to the MessageBox Subscription tables for routing as the promoted properties are; instead they are essentially XPath aliases (easy pointer or an abstraction of the XPATH query), which simply point to the appropriate XML data field.

To distinguish fields, you just need to right-click the node you want to mark, select **Promote**, and then **Show Promotions**.

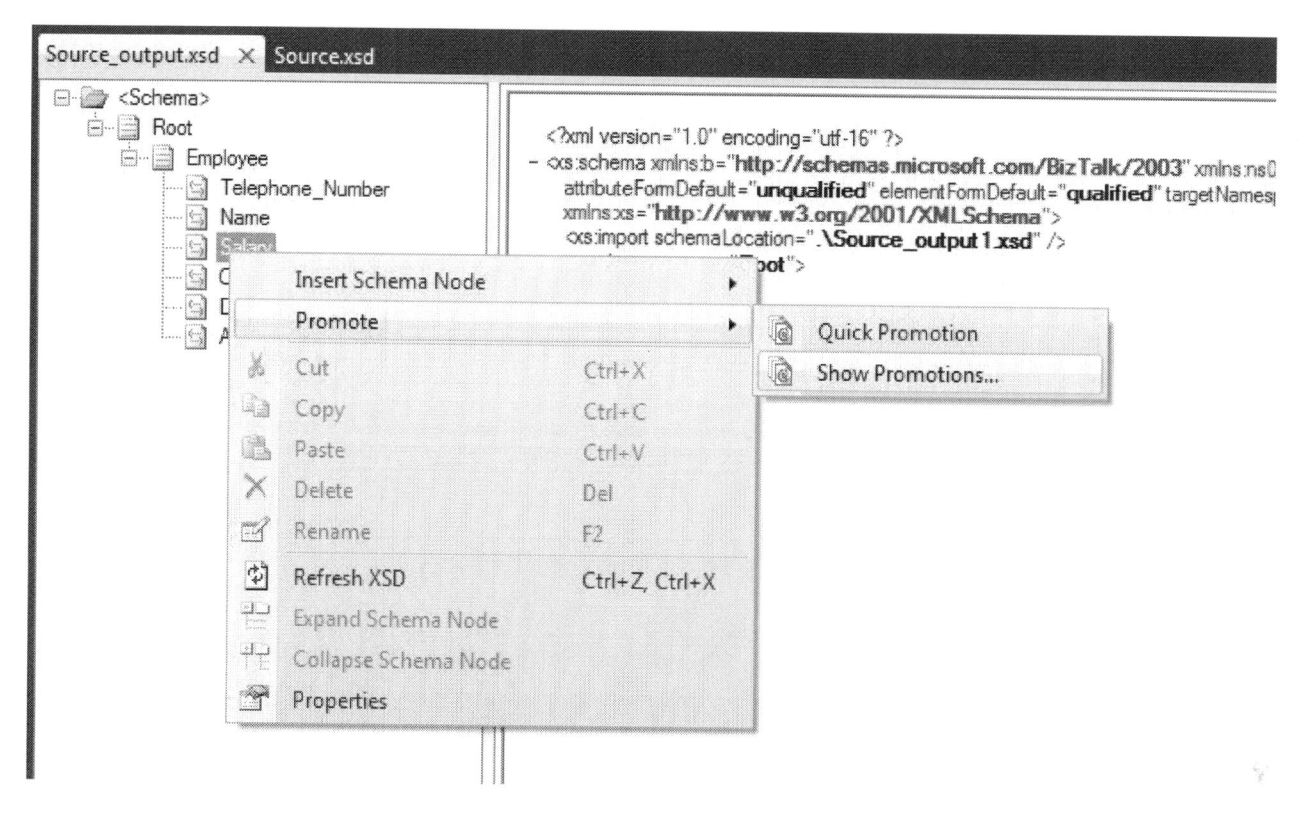

Figure 24: Show Promotions

When the Promotions screen is open, select the node you want to distinguish, select the **Distinguished Fields** tab, and then click **Add**. Figure 25 shows an example of this operation. For this example, we will be using the Salary attribute.

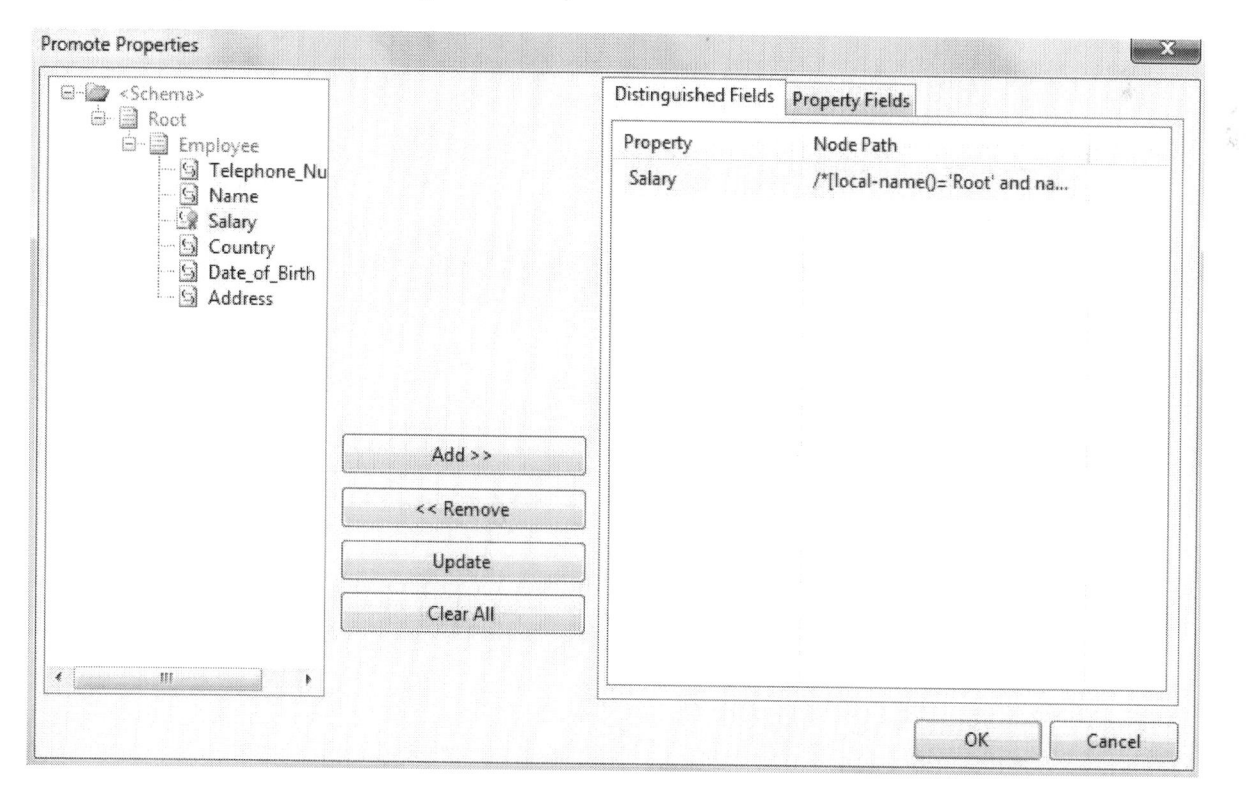

Figure 25: Distinguish salary node

Promoted Properties

The main difference between distinguished and promoted properties is the contexts in which they can be used. While distinguished properties are used to set or get values from messages inside orchestrations, promoted properties are used to route messages based in their values. They allow the Messaging Engine to route messages based on their value, and being in the message context allows doing so without having to look at the message payload. Promoted properties are the most common way to enable content-based routing. They are available to the pipelines, adapters, Message Bus, and orchestrations.

The best way to promote a field is to use the Quick Promotion option (in the same menu as Show Promotion). With this option, BizTalk will automatically create the promoted property in the property schema defined in the Default Property Schema Name of the schema property. If this is not present in our project, Visual Studio will automatically generate and add a property schema to your project.

Chapter 6 Mappings

Introduction

In a very simple way, a map (.BTM file) is a transformation from one Extensible Markup Language (XML) document into another XML document or more XML documents using a transformations language called XSLT. These maps are used in BizTalk in the following places:

- Receive ports
- Send ports
- Inside orchestrations

Maps are a core concept of BizTalk; they are responsible for making any necessary transformations in the message's data, which are exchanged by the different systems you want to integrate. These maps are developed inside Visual Studio 2010 using the BizTalk Mapper tool. This tool has a developer-friendly interface, which allows you to have a tree structure view of both input and output schemas used by the map.

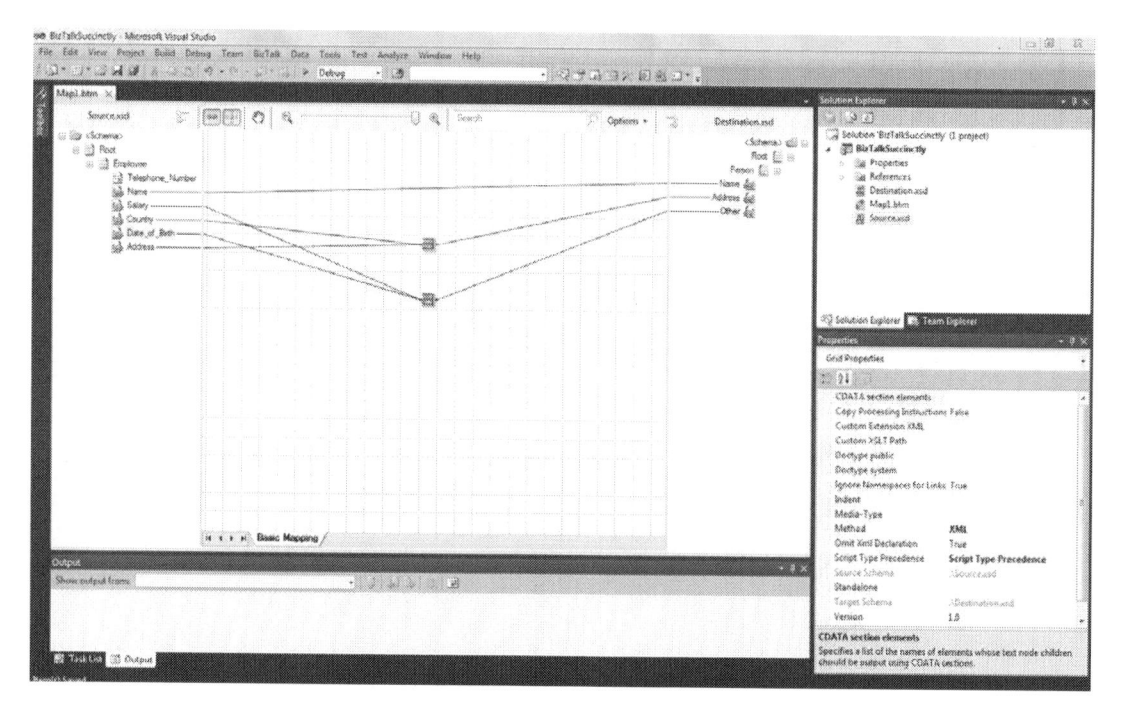

Figure 26: BizTalk Mapper Tool

Mapper Overview

The Mapper Editor is organized into seven distinct areas, each representing different behaviors and configurations for the map and schema nodes. The available areas are:

1. The **Functoids** panel, which has all the available functoids for you to use in the map.
2. The **Grid** panel, which is where all your mappings and transformations are represented. For a logical organization, BizTalk allows you to separate your mappings into pages, which are available in the bottom of the grid.
3. The **source schema structure**. This represents your incoming messages for this map. Have all nodes available for you to map and transform.
4. The **destination schema structure**. This represents your outgoing messages for this map. Have all nodes available from where you will map the transformed nodes.
5. The **Output** panel. This is where you will see the result of your map validations and testing. This tool is a very important form of debugging, which you might already know from your .NET projects.
6. The **Solution Explorer**. This is a common panel for all Visual Studio projects. It represents the solution structure for your BizTalk application.
7. The **Properties** window. This is also a shared window for all Visual Studio projects. It shows all available properties for the selected object.

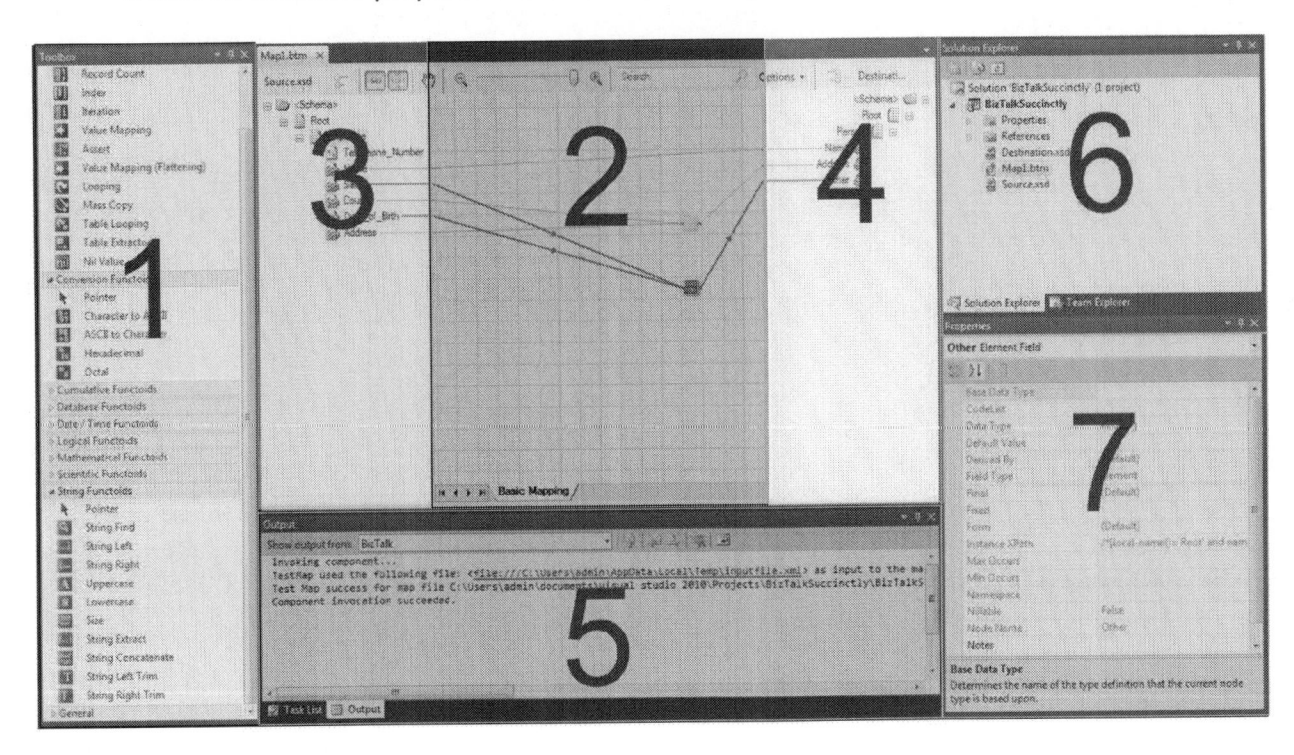

Figure 27: Mapper overview

Adding a Map to the Project

Adding maps to your project is very easy, as maps are SDK artifacts. To add a map, right-click your project in the Solution Explorer and select **Add** > **Add New Item** and then select **Map**. Don't forget to give it a descriptive name in the **Add New Item** screen. Once you add the new map, BizTalk will open the mapping editor without any schemas and transformations, as you can see in Figure 28.

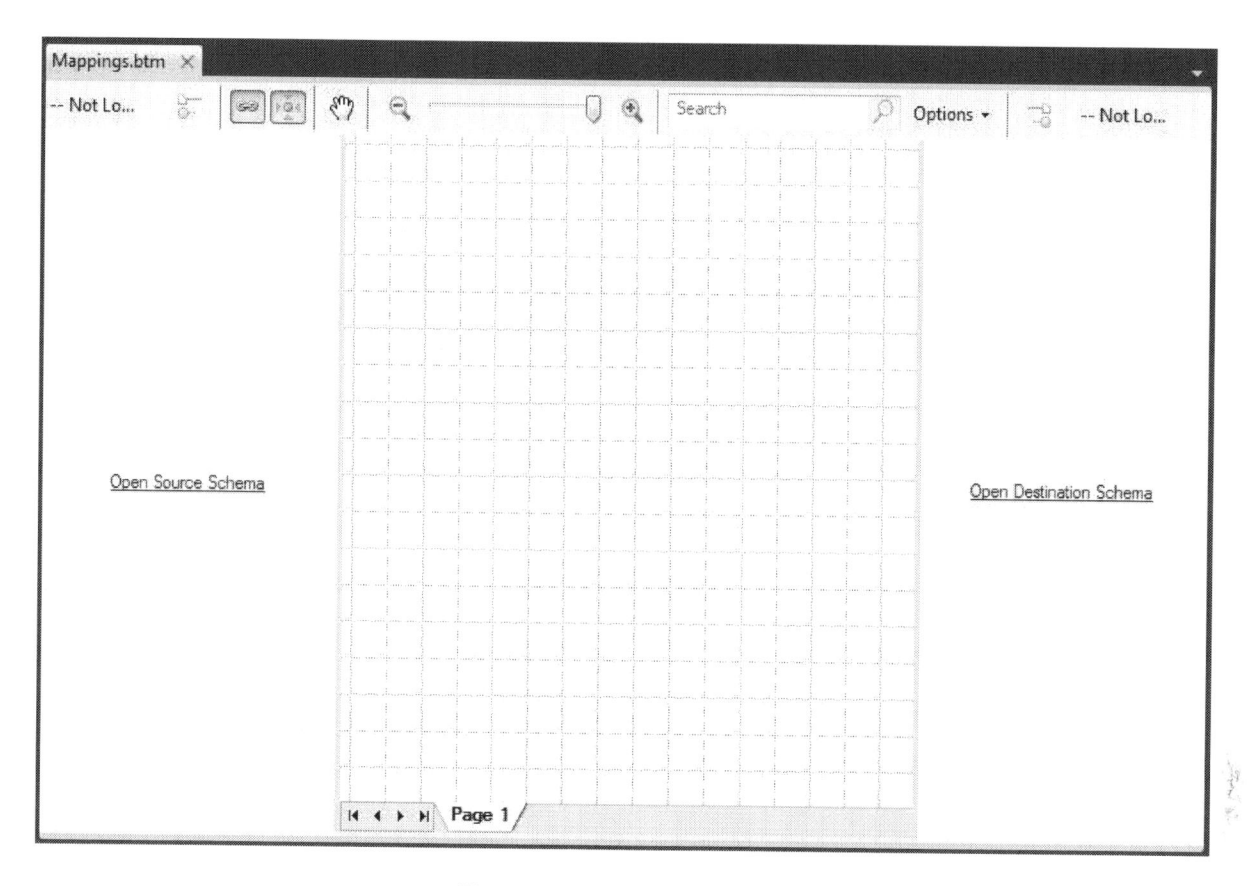

Figure 28: Empty maps

After you create your empty map, it's time to add your source and destination schema to it in order to start your mapping and transformations. It's important to recap that both schemas should now be already created or added to your project.

Add the Schemas to the Map

As you saw in Figure 28, the empty map has links in both source and destination schema that allow you to select schemas not only from your project, but also from any other project you reference in your solution. When you click on either **Open Source Schema** or **Open Destination Schema**, you will be prompted to choose the location of your schema.

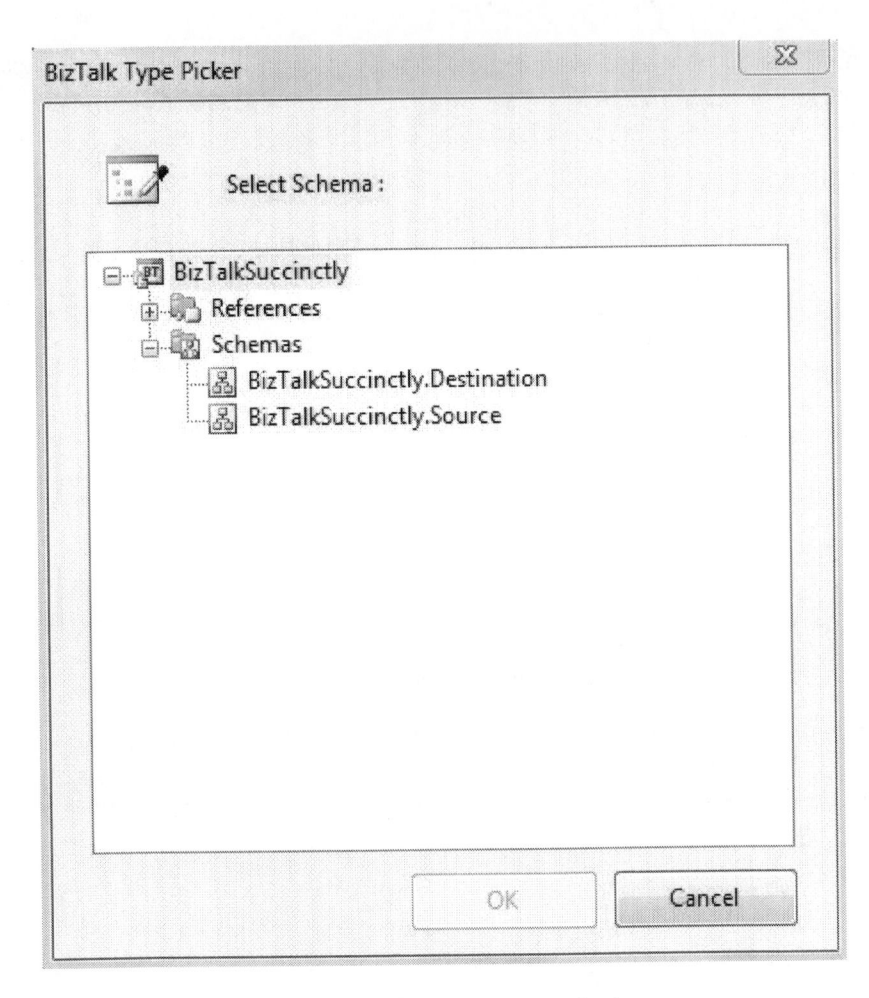

Figure 29: Add Schemas to project

For our example, we will add our **BizTalkSuccinctly.Source** schema as the source schema and the **BizTalkSuccinctly.Destination** as our destination schema. It is important for you to notice that we have configured our schemas with the namespace **BizTalkSuccinctly**, so BizTalk created two new types of messages with this namespace concatenated with the schema name, creating what is called the Fully Qualified Name of the schema. This is used to identify the type of messages subscribed by a subscriber.

Link Nodes

After adding your source and destination schema to the map, you can start implementing simple transformation rules by linking nodes from the source to the destination schema. A link is the way you associate a data item in the source schema with a data item in the destination schema. Typically, in a completed map there are many links between the source schema and the destination schema. All together the links specify how the data in the source instance messages will be transformed into semantically equivalent, but syntactically distinct, destination instance messages.

Linking nodes in BizTalk is a very simple operation, a drag and drop event that will automatically create a link between one source node and another destination node. To link nodes, click and drag the pointer of your mouse to the destination node. Figure 30 represents the link between two nodes in the map.

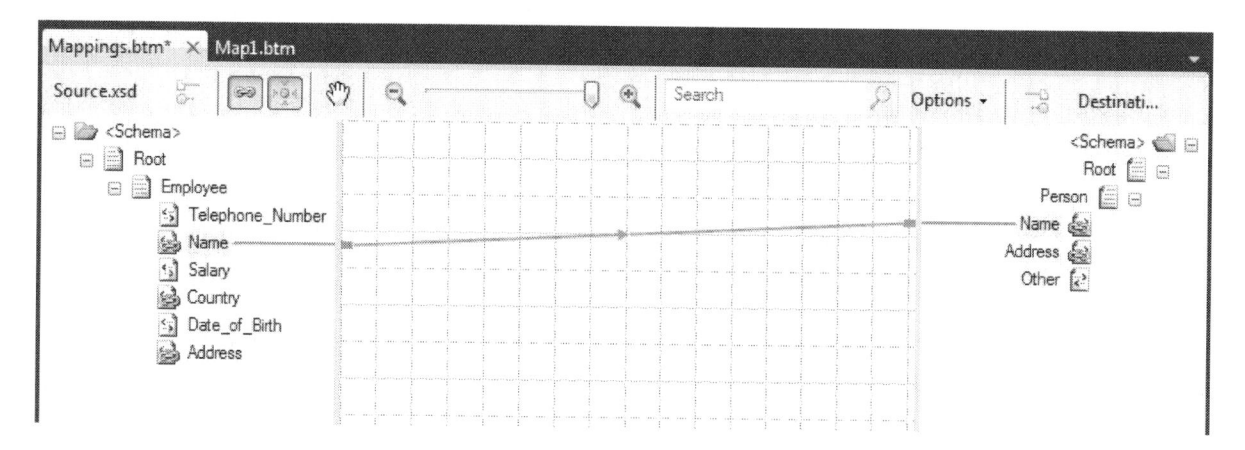

Figure 30: Linking nodes

BizTalk also provides you mechanisms to accelerate your mappings. In this case we are just mapping one node, but imagine you have source and destination schemas with hundreds of nodes and they all have the same names—we would lose our minds linking them all one by one. To accelerate the mapping, you can click **CTRL** while performing your link; when you finish the drag and drop, BizTalk will present you the following options:

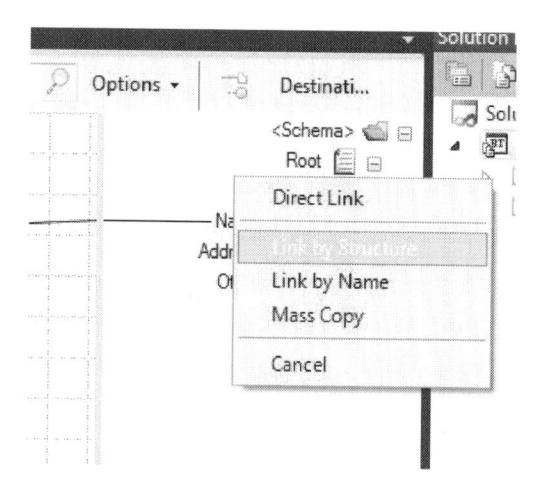

Figure 31: Link option

These options might become your best friends in node mappings, as they will spare you a lot of time. Table 4 summarizes these link options.

Table 4: Link Options

Name	Description
Direct Link	Using this technique, the BizTalk Mapper links the record from source schema to the selected record in the destination schema.

Name	Description
Link by Name	Using this technique, the BizTalk Mapper attempts to match the Record and Field nodes within the Record nodes being linked according to the names of the corresponding nodes, regardless of their structure, within the Record nodes being linked.
Link by Structure	Using this technique, the BizTalk Mapper attempts to match the Record and Field nodes within the Record nodes being linked according to the structures of those Record nodes, regardless of names of the corresponding nodes within those structures.
Mass Copy	The Mass Copy functoid enables your maps to use schemas that include any and anyAttribute elements.

Let's use the Link by Name option, for example. Figure 32 shows you the result of mapping just one node using this option; both nodes were linked automatically.

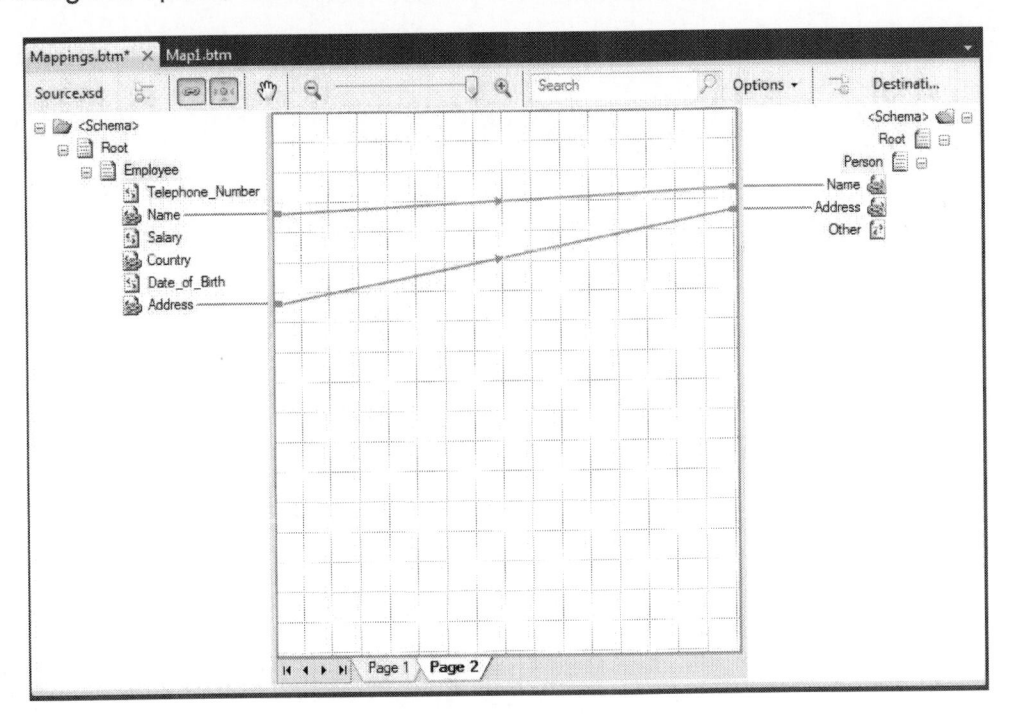

Figure 32: Links by Name

Functoids

Sometimes, direct links in a BizTalk map are not enough to respect the destination schema format, and we need to apply some data translation or transformation. It could be the concatenation or the cast of a node to a specific type, and several operations might be needed to fulfill those destination schema's requirements.

Functoids are the response to this problem, encapsulating the transformation logics used to perform all the required processing over source node values to work with the destination node format and values. BizTalk has many functoids, which can be as simple as concatenating string to multiply values or loop through repetitive records inside an XML file.

Inside the mapper you can find all available functoids in the toolbox, which you can identify in the left side of your map editor tool. When you open the toolbox, you will find these functoids divided into categories that represent the type of operations to which that functoid responds.

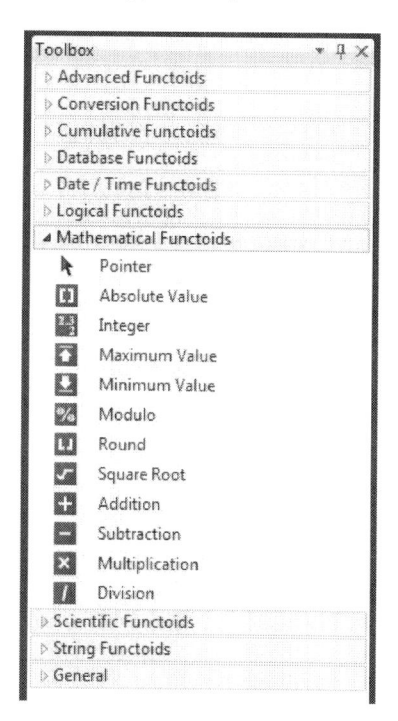

Figure 33: Functoids categories

Once you identify the functoid you want to use, the process of adding it to your map and configuring its behavior is the same for all functoids; you just need to drag and drop the functoid into the map, link the source node/nodes to the functoid, double-click it to configure any additional settings, and link the functoid to the destination node.

In the following example, we want to concatenate the address of an employee with the country, but separate it with a semicolon and then connect it to a destination node. The first step is to add our concatenate functoid by dragging it to the center of the map, as you can see in the Figure 34.

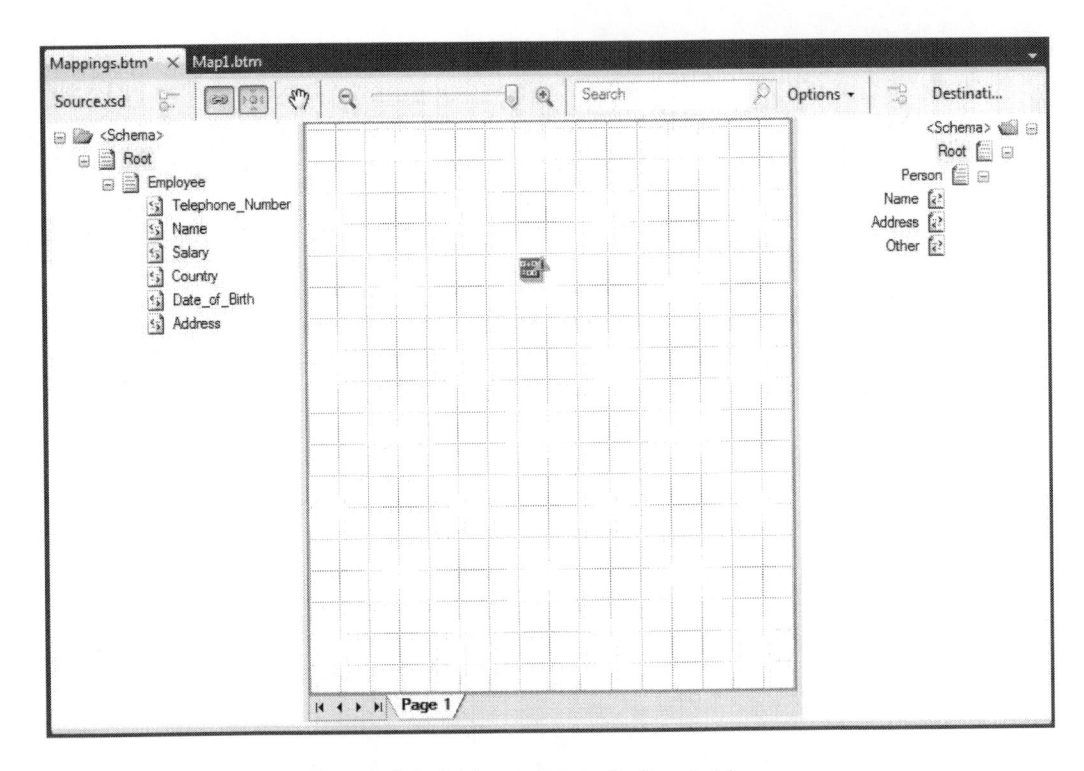

Figure 34: Add concatenate functoid

After you add the concatenate functoid, BizTalk will put a warning on top of it, which indicates that the functoid has no output nodes. It is important for you to understand that a functoid might not need input nodes, but it must link to at least one output node. Now we need to link both the Address and Country nodes to the concatenate functoid, and link the functoid to the destination node. As you can see in Figure 35, the warning no longer exists.

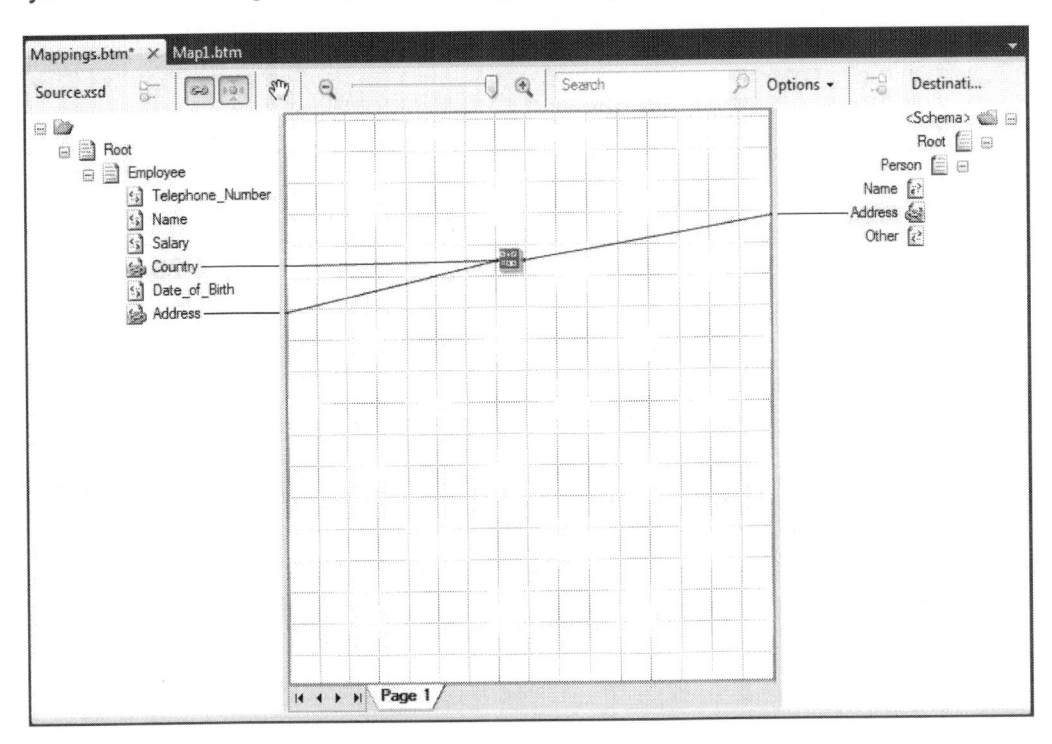

Figure 35: Properly linked functoid

Lastly, you need to add the semicolon as the separator between both nodes. To do so, double-click on top of the functoid and you will see the configuration screen. Please keep in mind that all functoids have this behavior; if you need to configure any additional setting, double-click it and configure what you need. After you double-click it, you will see something like Figure 36, in which you can see that I added the semicolon between the nodes.

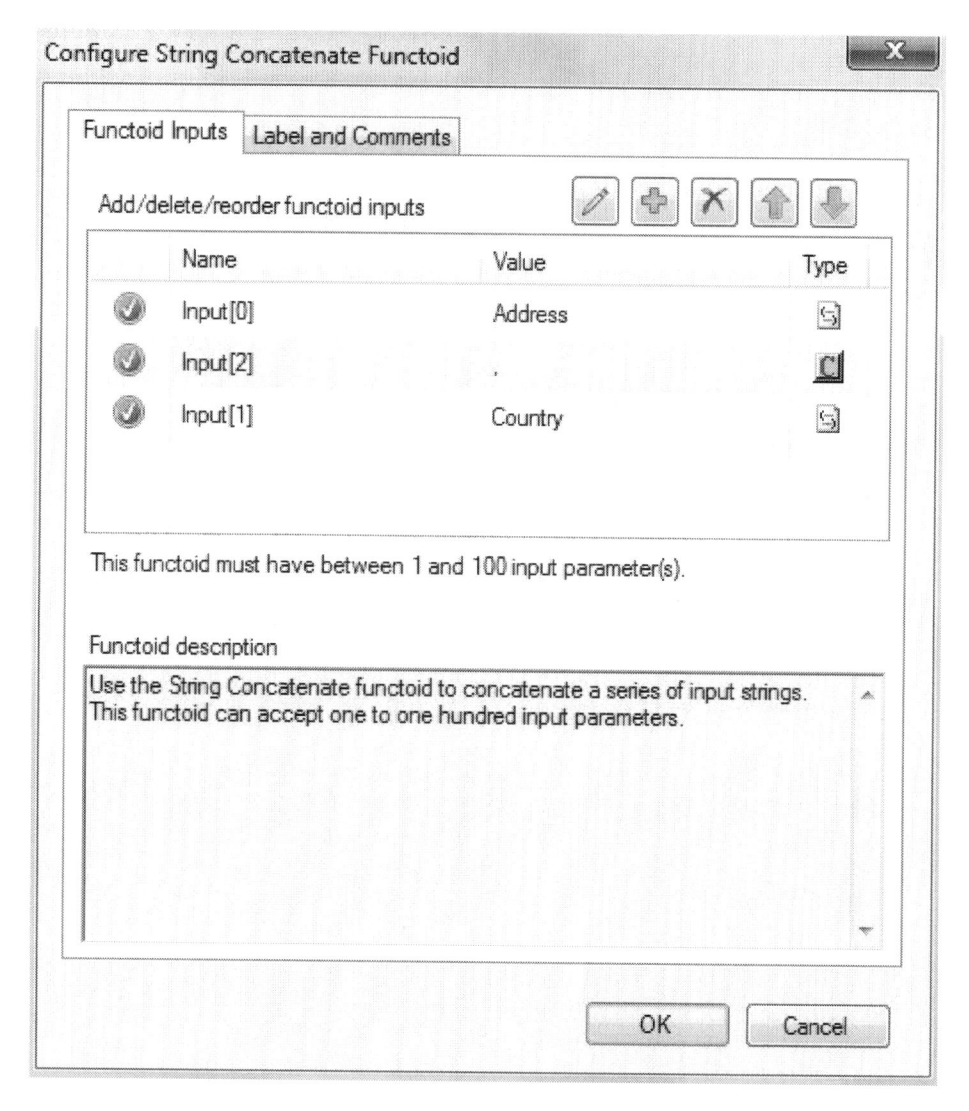

Figure 36: Setting up the concatenate functoid

This functoid not only allows you to add strings to your concatenation logics, it also allows you to reorder the nodes or even remove some nodes or strings from it.

This BizTalk functoid mechanism allows developers to maintain and develop mappings and message transformations very easily.

Available Functoids

Although the concatenate functoid is easy to use, there are others that are much more complex. The following tables will show you all available out-of-the-box functoids and their categories.

String Functoids

This category of functoid represents all available functoids for string manipulation. All of these functoids have a string as a return object, and their inputs might be an input node from the source schema or a static string, configured as an input parameter in the functoid configuration screen. The available functoids in this category are described in Table 5.

Table 5: String Functoids

Shape	Name	Description
	String Find	Returns the first found instance of the second parameter inside the first parameter.
	String Left	Returns the number of characters specified in the second parameter from the left of the string.
	String Right	Returns the number of characters specified in the second parameter from the right of the string.
	Uppercase	Returns the input string in uppercase.
	Lowercase	Returns the input string in lowercase.
	Size	Returns an the length (int) of the input string.
	String Extract	Takes in three parameters (string, start, and end position) and returns a substring of the first input.
	String Concatenate	Takes in from one to 100 strings and returns the concatenation of them in the add order.
	Left Trim	Takes in a string and trims it from the left.
	Right Trim	Takes in a string and trims it from the right.

Advanced Functoids

This category of functoids allows you to perform advanced operations on their input. Some of them return an output that can be used as the input for another functoid or sent directly to the destination. In this category you have the following available functoids:

Table 6: Advanced Functoids

Shape	Name	Description
	Scripting	Allows you to execute custom code. Can be C#, Inline JScript .NET, Inline Visual Basic .NET, Inline XSLT, or Inline Call Template.
	Record Count	Returns the total occurrences of a node.
	Index	Using a node from the source schema as the first parameter and all other inputs as levels from the node, returns the value of the node indexed by the values from the other parameters.
	Iteration	Using as first parameter a node from the source schema, returns the iteration of the node, representing the current occurrence number of the node.
	Value Mapping	Outputs its first parameter if a second one is true.
	Assert	Allows you to make sure some conditions are always true, like assertions in normal C# code.
	Value Mapping (Flattenning)	This functoid differs from the Value Mapping functoid in that it attempts to flatten the input into the output.
	Looping	Using as input a node from source schema, iterates trhough its occurrences. Must connect to a destination node.
	Mass Copy	Recursively copies all nodes bellow the source node (input) to the destination node.
	Table Looping	Builds a table in memory useful for creating records in the output that have some structure that is not present in the input.
	Table Extractor	This functoid takes in two parameters: the first must be a Table Looping functoid, and the second is a number that indicates the column from the table to get the value from.
	Nil Value	Allows you to return null values if the input is true.

Conversion Functoids

This category of functoids allows you to perform conversions over input parameters and use the return output as the input for another functoid, or to be sent directly to the destination schema. In this category you have the following available functoids:

Table 7: Conversion Functoids

Shape	Name	Description
	ASCII to Charater	Returns the number converted into the character that has this number in the ASCII table
	Character to ASCII	Returns the first character of the input parameter (string) converted into the ASCII representation
	Hexadecimal	Returns the integer part of the input converted to an hexadecimal value. The input is assumed to be decimal.
	Octal	Returns the integer part of the input converted to an octal value. The input is assumed to be decimal.

Cumulative Functoids

Cumulative functoids allow you to perform operations on reoccurring nodes in the source schema and output one value based on all the occurrences of the input node. In this category you have the following available functoids:

Table 8: Cumulative Functoids

Shape	Name	Description
	Cumulative Average	Performs an average calculation over the input values, returning the result as a decimal value
	Cumulative Concatenate	Concatenates all occurrences of the string input, returning the output as one string
	Cumulative Maximum	Returns the maximum value over the amount of input values
	Cumulative Minimum	Returns the minimum value over the amount of input values
	Cumulative Sum	Returns the sum of all input values

Database Functoids

This functoid category allows you to perform lookup operations over databases in order to get stored values from it, and then adds and uses them in your mappings. In this category you have the following available functoids:

Table 9: Database functoids

Shape	Name	Description
	Database lookup	Has four inputs, a lookup value (typically an ID), a connection string, and the name of the table to look up, and the column name to find the value with that ID. BizTalk will then query the database and return the row found.
	Error return	Using what the database lookup functoid has input, returns any error that occured while performing the query against the database.
	Value extractor	Has two inputs, the database lookup functoid and a column name from the dataset extracted, and then returns the value for that column.
	Format Message	Returns a formatted and localized string using argument substitution and, potentially, ID and value cross-referencing.
	Get application ID	Retrieves an identifier for an application object.
	Get application value	Retrieves an application value.
	Get common ID	Retrieves an identifier for a common object.
	Get common value	Retrieves a common value.
	Remove application ID	Removes the identifier for an application object.
	Set common ID	Sets and returns an identifier for a common object.

Date/Time Functoids

These types of functoids allow you to perform date/time operations over input parameters or generate date/time object types to add to a destination node. Their output can be used as the input for another functoid or sent directly to the destination. In this category you have the following available functoids:

Table 10: Date/Time functoids

Shape	Name	Description
	Add days	Uses their two input parameters and returns a new date as a result of adding the number of days specified in the second parameter to the date specified in the first parameter.
	Date	Returns the current date, having no input parameters.
	Time	Returns the current time, having no input parameters.
	Date and Time	Returns the current date and time, having no input parameters.

Logical Functoids

This category of functoids performs logical operations on their input and returns a Boolean value that can be used later on as the input for another functoid or to instruct the compiler how to construct the generated XSLT. They are commonly used to define rules inside the mappings.

Table 11: Logical functoids

Shape	Name	Description
	Greater than	Returns true if the first parameter is greater than the second, false otherwise.
	Greater Than Or Equal	Returns true if the first parameter is greater than or equal the second, false otherwise.
	Less than	Returns true if the first parameter is less than the second, false otherwise.
	Less Than Or Equal	Returns true if the first parameter is less than or equal the second, false otherwise.
	Equal	Returns true if both parameters are equal, false otherwise.
	Not Equal	Returns true if the parameters are not equal, false otherwise.
	Logical String	Returns true the input parameter is a string, false otherwise.
	Logical Date	Returns true the input parameter is a date, false otherwise.

Shape	Name	Description
#	Logical Numeric	Returns true the input parameter is a numeric, false otherwise.
‖	Logical Or	Returns the logical OR over all input parameters.
&	Logical And	Returns the logical AND over all input parameters.
?	Logical Existence	Returns the evaluation of the node existence.
!	Logical NOT	Return the negation of a value of a Boolean.
	IsNil	Returns true if the node is set to nil in the schema, false otherwise.

Mathematical Functoids

These functoids are pretty much your transformation calculator; they allow you to perform mathematical operations on their input and return an output that can be used as the input for another functoid or sent directly to the destination schema. In this category you have the following available functoids:

Table 12: Mathematical functoids

Shape	Name	Description
	Absolute value	Takes in one value and it returns the absolute value of the value.
	Integer	Takes in one parameter and returns the integer part of the value, effectively removing the decimal point and all decimals.
	Maximum Value	Takes in a minimum of two parameters and a maximum of 100 parameters and, returns the highest of the values.
	Minimum Value	Takes in a minimum of two parameters and a maximum of 100 parameters, and returns the lowest of the values.
%	Modulo	Returns the remainder from performing a division of one first parameter by one second parameter.
	Round	Takes two parameters and returns the first rounded by the amount of decimal places defined by the second.

Shape	Name	Description
√	Square Root	Returns the square root of an input parameter.
+	Addition	Sums the parameters and returns the result.
−	Subtraction	Subtracts the parameters and returns the result.
×	Multiplication	Multiplies the parameters and returns the result.
/	Division	Divides the parameters and returns the result.

Scientific Functoids

These functoids are used to perform scientific mathematical operations on their input, and return an output that can be used as the input for another functoid or sent directly to the destination schema. These are complements to the mathematical category functoids and they are separated because they represent advanced mathematical operations. In this category you have the following available functoids:

Table 13: Scientific functoids

Shape	Name	Description
	Arc Tangent	Returns the result of performing the arc tangent function on the parameter
	Cosine	Returns the result of performing the cosine function on the parameter
a^b	X^Y	Returns the first input lifted to the power of the second input (Ex: 23^7)
	Sine	Returns the result of performing the sine function on the parameter
	Tangent	Returns the result of performing the tangent function on the parameter
e^n	Natural Exponential Function	Returns the base for the natural logarithm lifted to the power of the parameter.
Ln	Natural Logarithm	Returns the natural logarithm of the parameter
10^n	10^n	Returns 10 lifted to the power of the parameter (Ex: 10^4)

Shape	Name	Description
Log 10	Common Logarithm	Returns the 10-based logarithm of the parameter
Log n	Base-Specified Logarithm	Returns the base-specified logarithm function using the second parameter as base and performing the function on the first parameter

Maps Operations in Visual Studio

Test Map

While developing our maps, we will perform transformations to input schemas in order to respect our output schemas. This means that every XML document that will be received through our application Receive Ports or processed inside orchestrations will be transformed according to those same transformations.

As you can imagine, it would be dangerous to deploy our mappings without any previous testing, as we could be sending invalid messages to our trading partners. BizTalk provides a mechanism to simulate the execution of our map, based on an input XML or flat file document, and retrieve the expected XML or flat file inside Visual Studio. You can also check and inspect the XSLT generated by the mapper engine. It is important to understand that although BizTalk validates the XSLT structure and syntax, it's your job as a developer to validate if the resulting XML document respects the requirements from your trading partner.

To use this tool, you just need to right-click your map in the Solution Explorer and choose the **Test Map** option.

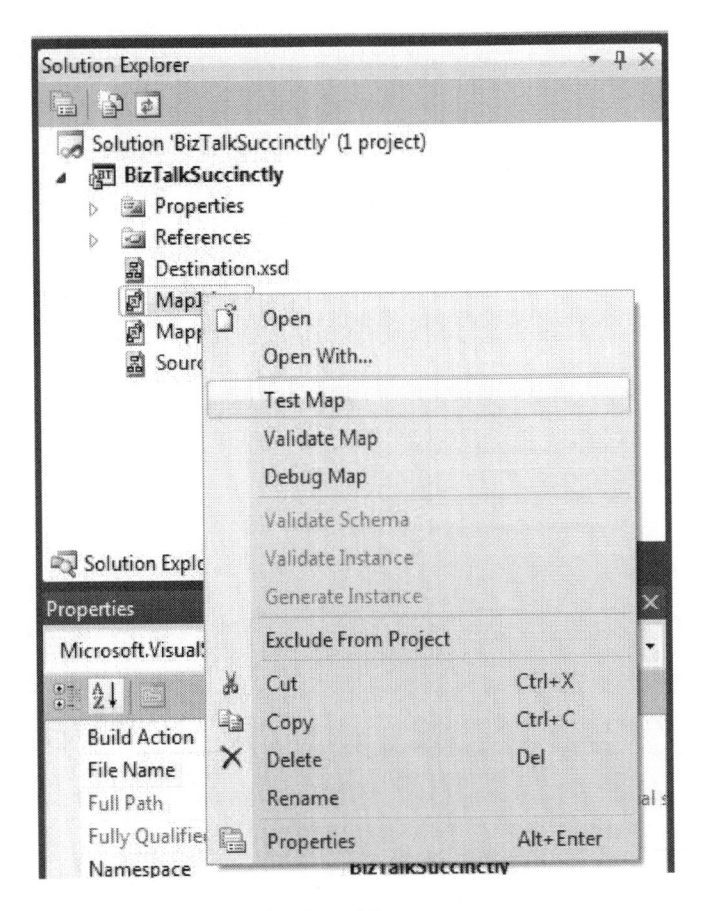

Figure 37: Test Map menu

BizTalk will then generate an output document, which you can access by clicking in the file location in the output windows.

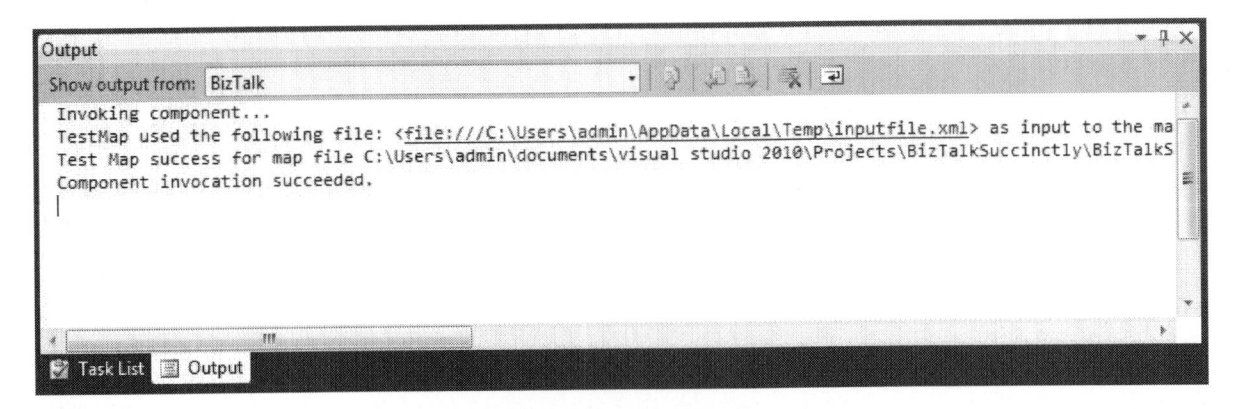

Figure 38: Test Map

Although you can use this tool directly with no customization, the map properties allow you to execute tests on different conditions, such as a custom input XML to test against real sample scenarios. To do so, you can access the map properties and change the property **Test Map Input** to **XML** and then configure your test XML file path in the **Test Map Input Instance** property.

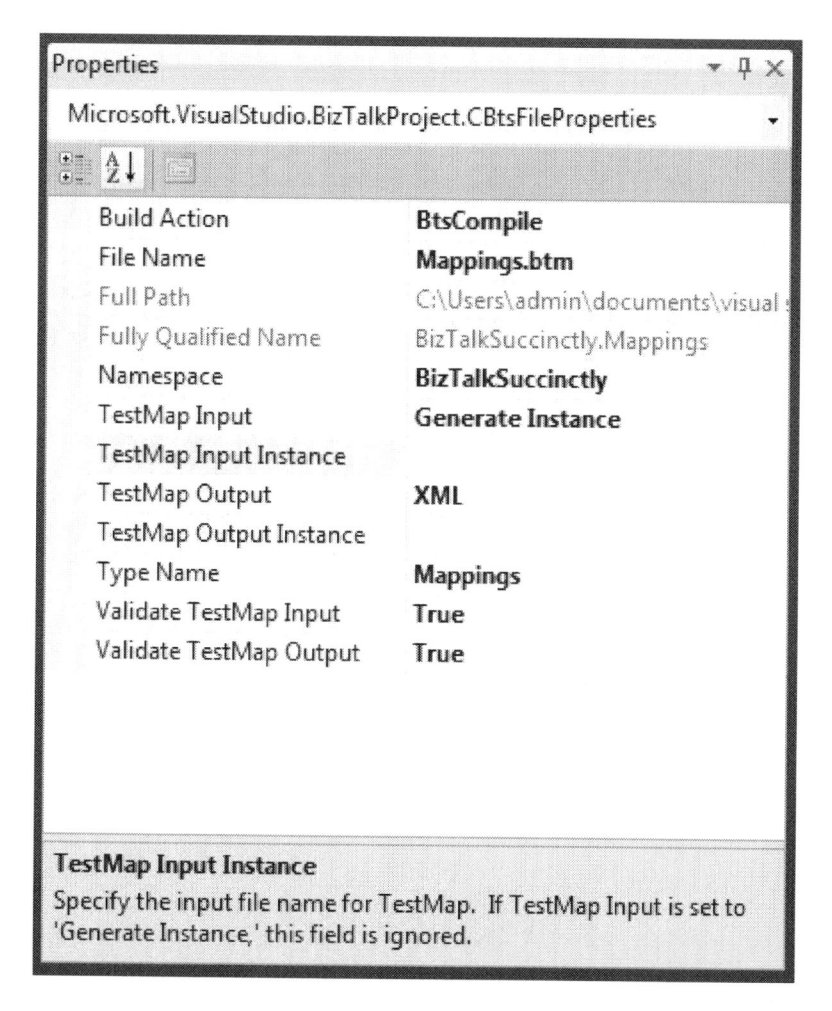

Figure 39: Custom Test Map Executions

Validate Map

Map validation is a simple operation commonly used while developing BizTalk mapping. While testing maps helps you visualize the result of a mapping transformation over an XML document, this feature validates the consistency of your transformation (for example, if there is a required node that is not linked, or if you have multiple links to the same node). To use this option, right-click your map in the Solution Explorer and choose **Validate Map**.

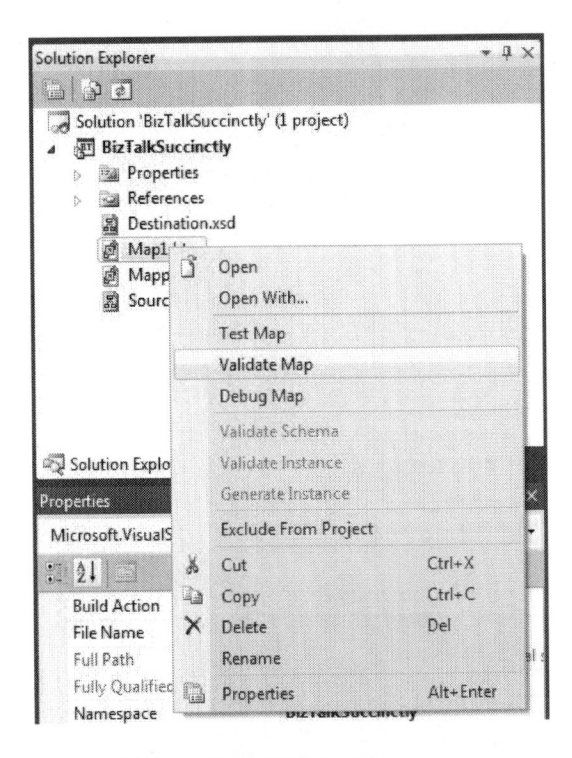

Figure 40: Validate Map

After the execution of the map validation ends, BizTalk will generate an output indicating if there are errors or warnings, or none if it was successful, and the XSLT generated to perform the mappings. This XSLT will be provided to you either in case of success or not. Look for the line in the output window that has the path to it and you can open it:

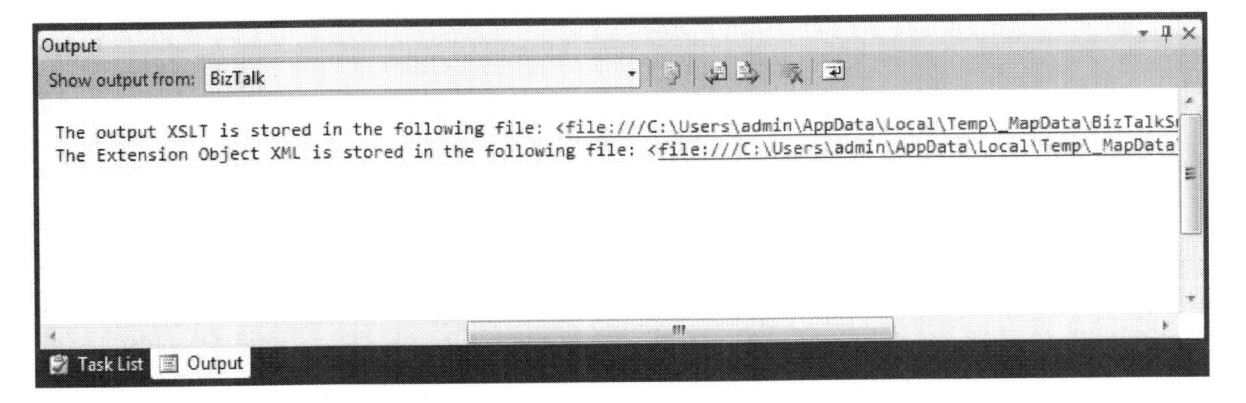

Figure 41: Output of XSLT document

One you open the file, the syntax will be familiar if you have already worked with XSLT documents. It has all the nodes from the schema used as output and for each one the logics of transformation, as well as the XPath reference used to get the required node from the source schema.

```xml
<?xml version="1.0" encoding="UTF-16" ?>
<xsl:stylesheet xmlns:xsl="http://www.w3.org/1999/XSL/Transform" xmlns:msxsl="urn:schemas-microsoft-com:xslt" xmlns:var="http://schemas.microsoft.com/BizTalk/2003/var" exclude-result-prefixes="msxsl var s0 userCSharp" version="1.0" xmlns:s0="http://BizTalkSuccinctly.Source" xmlns:ns0="http://BizTalkSuccinctly.Destination" xmlns:userCSharp="http://schemas.microsoft.com/BizTalk/2003/userCSharp">
  <xsl:output omit-xml-declaration="yes" method="xml" version="1.0" />
  <xsl:template match="/">
    <xsl:apply-templates select="/s0:Root" />
  </xsl:template>
  <xsl:template match="/s0:Root">
    <xsl:variable name="var:v1" select="userCSharp:StringConcat(string(Employee/Address/text()) , &quot;,&quot; , string(Employee/Country/text()))" />
    <xsl:variable name="var:v2" select="userCSharp:StringConcat(string(Employee/Salary/text()) , string(Employee/Date_of_Birth/text()))" />
    <ns0:Root>
      <Person>
        <Name>
          <xsl:value-of select="Employee/Name/text()" />
        </Name>
        <Address>
          <xsl:value-of select="$var:v1" />
        </Address>
        <Other>
          <xsl:value-of select="$var:v2" />
        </Other>
      </Person>
    </ns0:Root>
  </xsl:template>
```

Figure 42: Figure 1 XSLT Generation

As BizTalk is based on the .NET framework of Microsoft for its functoids, you will also find the blocks of C# code used for any transformations or programming logics. As I only used the Concatenation functoid in this map, the XSLT code only has the C# code function to execute its logic.

```
<msxsl:script language="C#" implements-prefix="userCSharp">
<![CDATA[
public string StringConcat(string param0, string param1, string param2)
{
    return param0 + param1 + param2;
}


public string StringConcat(string param0, string param1)
{
    return param0 + param1;
}




]]>
</msxsl:script>
```

Figure 43: Concatenate functoid C# code in XSLT

Debug Map

The debug option in the Map Editor is commonly used when validation and testing is not enough to find an error or to evaluate an output document. This way you can debug step-by-step the building of your XML document, through the execution of all mapping transformations defined in the map. This feature is pretty similar to any debug in C#/.NET application development, so if you are familiar with breakpoint, step into, and watchers, this is pretty much the same for you. To use this feature, right-click your map in the Solution Explorer and then select the **Debug Map** option, as you can see in Figure 44:

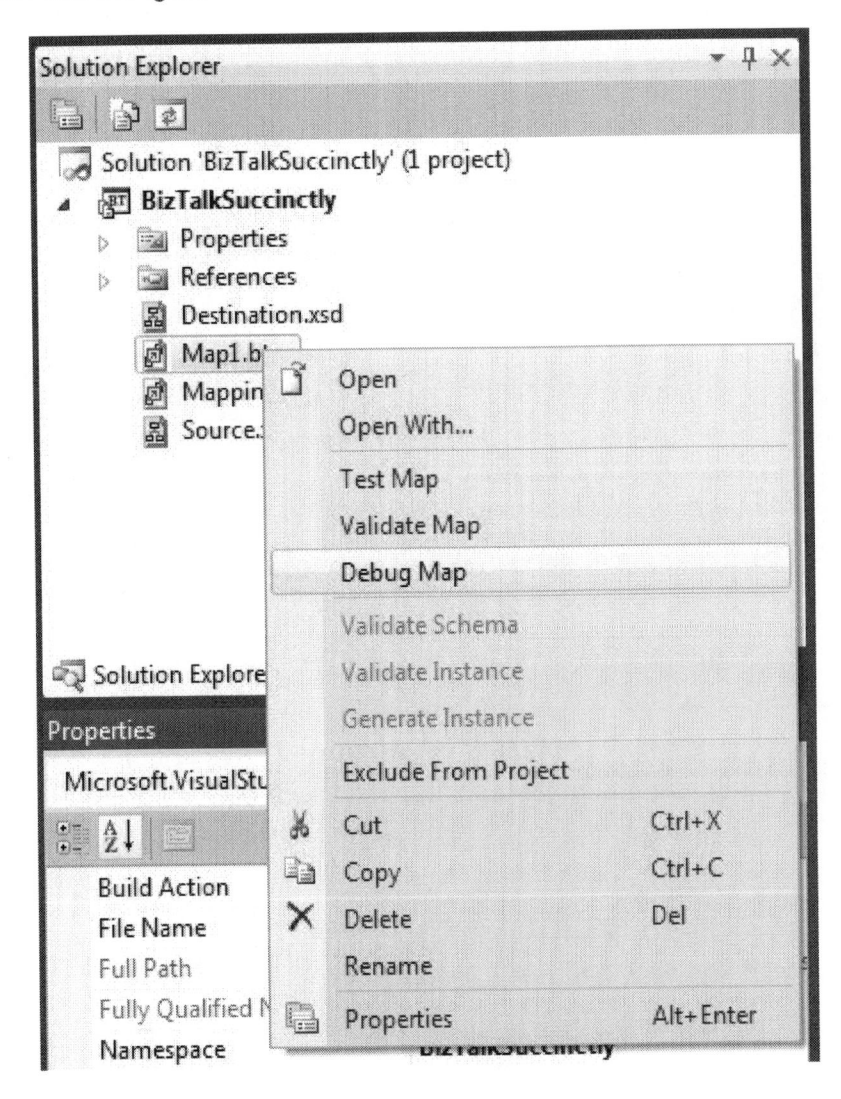

Figure 44: Debug Map

Once you click on the Debug Map option, BizTalk opens a new Window in which you can define breakpoints and watch the result of the step execution in a result panel. Figure 45 shows you this debug window.

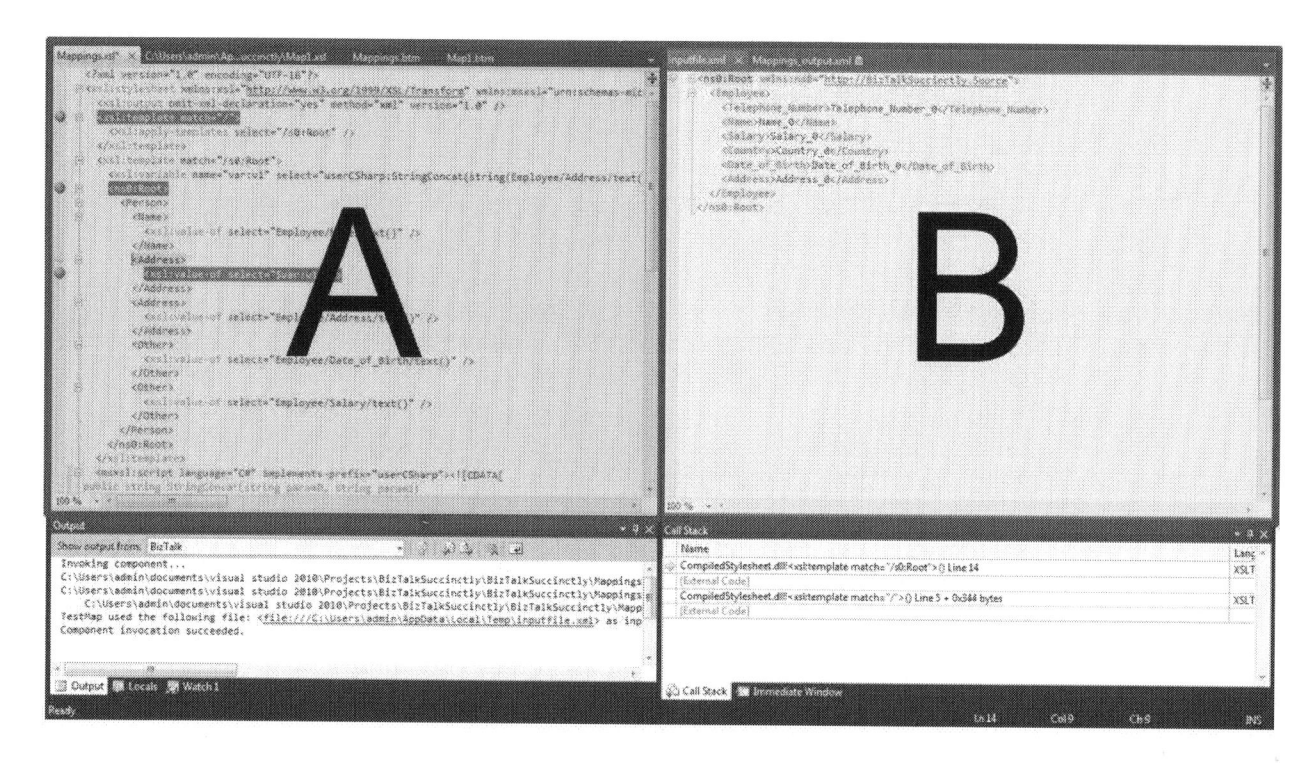

Figure 45: Debug Window

The previous figure shows you two separate panels inside this Debug Window. On panel A, based on the XSLT generated for your map, you can define your breakpoints (where the debugger will stop on the next execution). On panel B, you have the resulting panel in which your XML document is being created according to the step you are in in the XSLT code execution.

Chapter 7 Pipelines

Introduction

Pipelines are powerful BizTalk artifacts used to standardize inbound and outbound messages for pre-processing in receive ports or post-processing in send ports (for example, as parsing operations, validations, or schema evaluation before storing a message in MessageBox or sending a message to external systems or to a destination system). BizTalk divides pipelines into two distinct types: receive pipelines and send pipelines. These two types of pipelines differ from each other in the number of stages they have.

A receive pipeline has four different stages:

1. **Decode**—This stage is used to perform decoding or decryption of a message. This stage is used for components that decode or decrypt the message. The MIME/SMIME Decoder pipeline component or a custom decoding component should be placed in this stage if the incoming messages need to be decoded from one format to another.
2. **Disassemble**—This stage disassembles messages into XML format. Out-of-the-box BizTalk brings two disassemblers: XML and Flat File. This stage is used for components that validate the message format. A pipeline component processes only messages that conform to the schemas specified in that component. If a pipeline receives a message whose schema is not associated with any component in the pipeline, that message is not processed. Depending on the adapter that submits the message, the message is either suspended or an error is issued to the sender.
3. **Validate**—Validates the XML contents, verifying the schema conformance. This stage is used for components that validate the message format. A pipeline component processes only messages that conform to the schemas specified in that component. If a pipeline receives a message whose schema is not associated with any component in the pipeline, that message is not processed. Depending on the adapter that submits the message, the message is either suspended or an error is issued to the sender.
4. **Resolve Party**—Determines to which party this message will be sent after being transformed. This stage is a placeholder for the Party Resolution Pipeline Component.

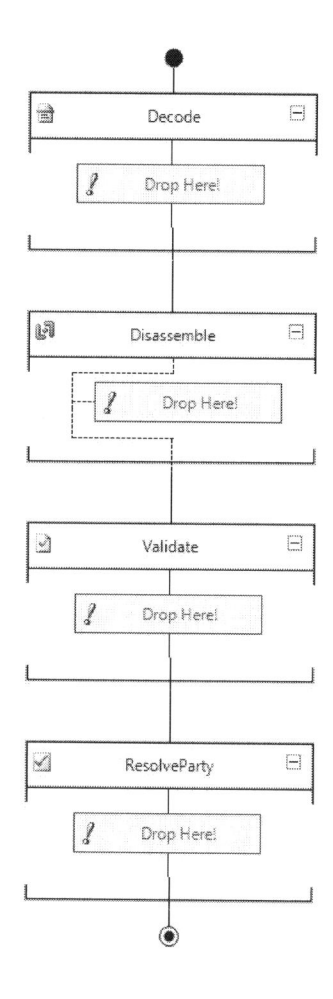

Figure 46: Receive Pipeline

Send pipelines will make the opposite of receive pipelines, making any post transformation processing's needed before sending it. If for instance your trading-partner requires a Flat File, BizTalk must transform its internal XML message format to this expected one. These pipelines consist of three stages:

1. **Pre-Assemble**—This is a custom stage, as BizTalk doesn't bring any out-of-the-box component. This stage is executed before the message enters the Pipeline. This stage is a placeholder for custom components that should perform some action on the message before the message is serialized.
2. **Assemble**—Converts the XML message into the flat file format needed. BizTalk brings two components for this stage, XML assembler and Flat File Assembler. Components in this stage are responsible for assembling or serializing the message and converting it to or from XML
3. **Encode**—Used for encrypting the message or adding any signature to it. BizTalk brings the MIME/SMIME encoder to use in this stage. This stage is used for components that encode or encrypt the message. Place the MIME/SMIME Encoder component or a custom encoding component in this stage if message signing is required.

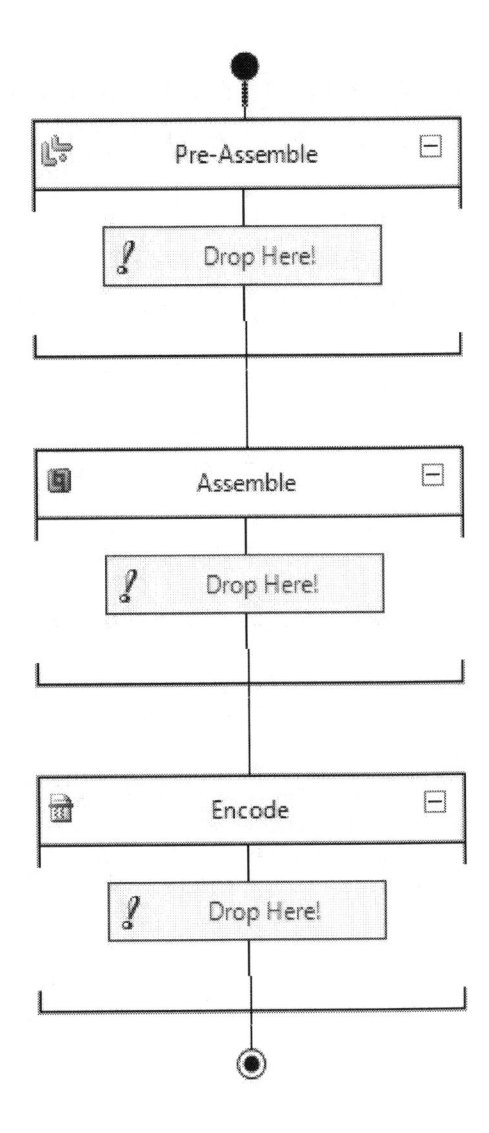

Figure 47: Send Pipeline

At this point you might be asking yourself why have I been talking about available components to use in these stages. This is because it's you as a developer that is responsible for developing any custom pipelines if needed, as BizTalk only brings four default pipelines to use in receive and send Pipelines, and these are meant for simple scenarios. They are the following:

PassThruReceive

This is a Pipeline meant to be applied to a receive port, and has no component in it. You can see an example of this Pipeline structure in Figure 47. It allows any message to enter your port without any processing.

XML Receive

This is a Pipeline meant to be applied to a receive port and has only the XML Disassembler and the Party Resolution component. This is a nice Pipeline for starts as it disassembles your XML input (must be XML) and evaluates which partners will receive it.

PassThruTransmit

This is a Pipeline meant to be applied to a send port and as no component in it. You can see an example of this Pipeline structure in Figure 48. Allsow any message to be sent through your port, and without any processing.

XML Transmit

This is a Pipeline meant to be applied to a send port, and has only the XML Assembler. If you are sending an XML document through your port without any post processing, keep in mind that BizTalk internal message format in XML, so a PassThruTransmit pipeline will be enough for you.

These Pipelines will become available when you start configuring your physical ports in the BizTalk administrator.

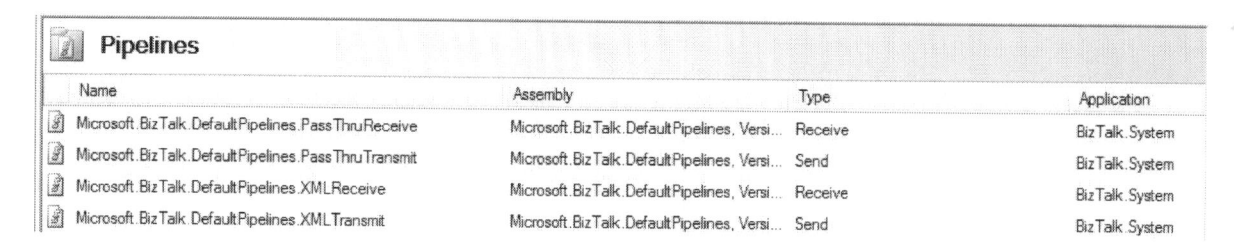

Figure 48: Available pipelines in BizTalk Administrator

Custom Pipelines

Developing custom pipelines is about adding components from those available in the Pipeline Editor to the available stages, according to your pipeline type (receive or send). To start creating your own pipelines, right-click in your project in Visual Studio, select **Add**, **New Item**, and select **Receive Pipeline** or **Send Pipeline**, according to your development needs. After that, BizTalk will show you the Pipeline Editor.

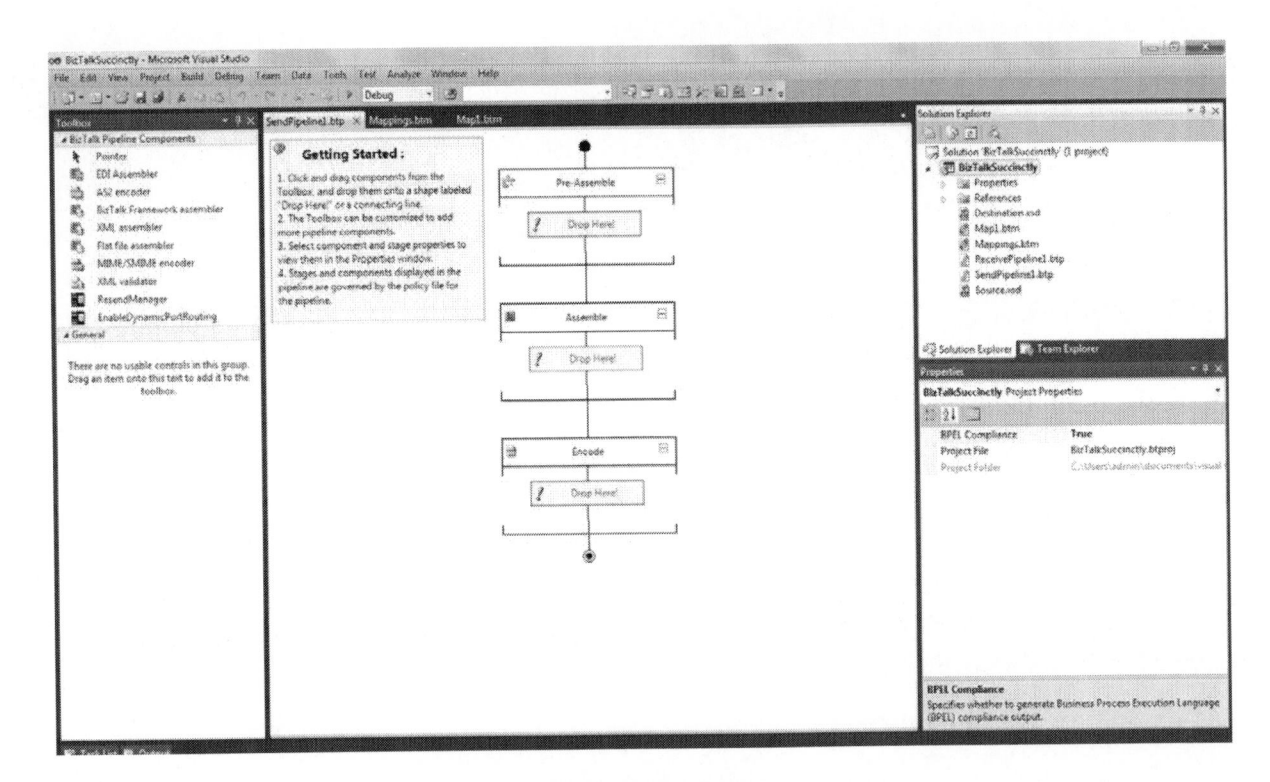

Figure 49: Pipeline Editors

In the toolbox, you will find all the components we have already talked about. To add them to their corresponding stage, just drag and drop them to the appropriate stage. After you drop the component, the stage will appear as shown in Figure 50.

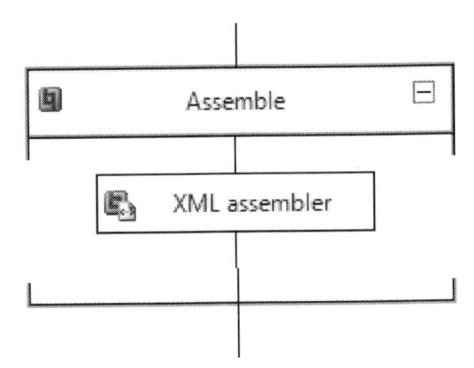

Figure 50: Pipeline Stage

Chapter 8 Orchestrations

Introduction

Orchestrations are an optional component in your BizTalk projects, as you can simply make a solution with orchestrations respond to integrations that required more complex logics or respond to business process flows.

In a very simple way, orchestrations are a representation of the business process in a visual way (the association of links between shapes, representation of ports, and some configurations) that can subscribe to (receive) and publish (send) messages through the MessageBox database, making it easier to manage and read than textual language (C#, Java). It simplifies the process of creating orchestration models of business processes that are compiled into executable code. Or, we can say that it is a BizTalk artifact representing an arbitrary portion of a business process.

Important benefits of using BizTalk orchestrations include:

- Handling different types of transactions.
- Better error handling.
- Defining correlation types between messages for asynchronous processes.

Adding an orchestration to your project is easy; just right-click your project in the Solution Explorer and select **Add > Add New Item > Orchestration**. BizTalk will open an Orchestration Editor so that you can start developing your orchestration.

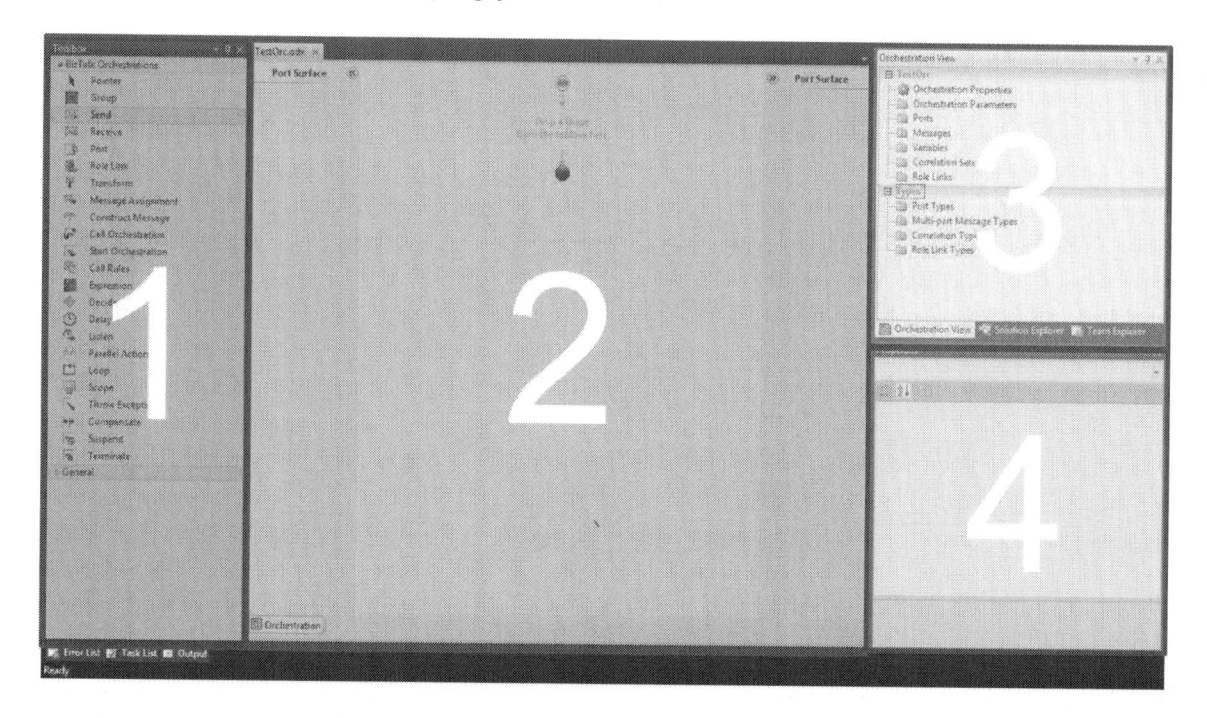

Figure 51: Orchestration Editor

As you can see in Figure 51, the Orchestration Editor is divided into four main work areas. These areas are:

Toolbox

This is where all the tools available to create the business logic of your orchestration (workflow) are available. Drag and drop them to the Orchestration Designer to use them.

Orchestration Designer

This is where you design your orchestration or your business process in a visual way. Using a drag-and-drop operation, you add the tools you need to build the orchestration. This is a very helpful component, as it allows you to see your orchestration workflow.

Orchestration Overview

This is where you can create your messages, port, variables, and any other allowed object to use inside the orchestration.

Properties Window

The Properties window is common to every Visual Studio-based project; it allows you to set selected object properties.

Available Shapes

The toolbox available for the Orchestration Editor displays multiple shapes for you to use in order to set up your business processes. With these shapes, you will be able to add intelligence to the business processes, applying business rules and conditions so that in runtime the messages take their correct flow. The following table shows you the available shapes in the toolbox.

Table 14: Available shapes for orchestrations

Shape	Name	Description
	Group	Enables you to group operations into a single collapsible and expandable unit for visual convenience.
	Send	Enables you to send a message from your orchestration.
	Receive	Enables you to receive a message in your orchestration.
	Port	Defines where and how messages are transmitted.

Shape	Name	Description
	Role Link	Enables you to create a collection of ports that communicate with the same logical partner, perhaps through different transports or endpoints.
	Transform	The Transform shape can only occur inside a Construct Message shape. Enables you to map the fields from existing messages into new messages.
	Message Assignment	The Message Assignment shape can only occur inside a Construct Message shape. Enables you to assign message values.
	Construct Message	Enables you to construct a message.
	Call Orchestration	Enables your orchestration to call another orchestration synchronously.

Table 15: Available shapes for orchestrations II

Shape	Name	Description
	Decide	Enables you to conditionally branch in your orchestration.
	Delay	Enables you to build delays in your orchestration based on a time-out interval.
	Listen	Enables your orchestration to conditionally branch depending on messages received or the expiration of a timeout period.
	Parallel Actions	Enables your orchestration to perform two or more operations independently of each other.
	Loop	Enables your orchestration to loop until a condition is met.
	Scope	Provides a framework for transactions and exception handling.
	Throw Exception	Enables you to explicitly throw an exception in the event of an error.
	Compensate	Enables you to call code to undo or compensate for operations already performed by the orchestration when an error occurs.

Table 16: Available tools for orchestrations III

Shape	Name	Description
	Start Orchestration	Enables your orchestration to call another orchestration asynchronously.
	Call Rules	Enables you to configure a Business Rules policy to be executed in your orchestration.
	Expression	Enables you to assign values to variables or make .NET calls.
	Suspend	Suspends the operation of your orchestration to enable intervention in the event of some error condition.
	Terminate	Enables you to immediately end the operation of your orchestration in the event of some error condition.

Creating a Simple Orchestration

We will be creating step-by-step a simple orchestration in which you receive a message, apply a pre-created map, and then send it through a send port. After creating the orchestration, we will deploy the project and set up the application with the BizTalk Server Administrator.

To create our Project, we must start with the input and output schemas. These are very simple as we are going to transform a schema containing records with just three elements (First Name, Middle Name, and Last Name) into a schema containing just one full name record. Our schemas are shown in Figures 52 and 53:

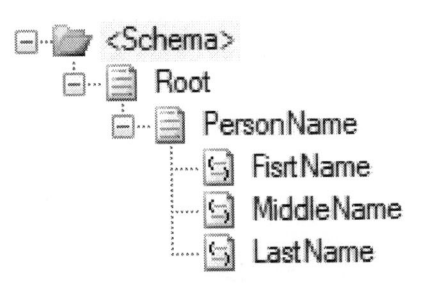

```
<Schema>
  Root
    PersonName
      FisrtName
      MiddleName
      LastName
```

Figure 52: Destination Schemas

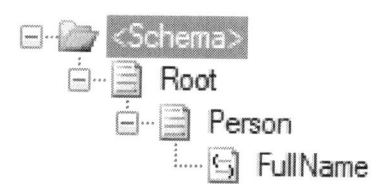

Figure 53: Source Schemas

Our map is going to be pretty simple as well. In the following map you can see that we will loop through all person records in the XML document and then evaluate if the name is a string, and if it is, map it to a concatenate functoid, and link the result of the concatenate functoid with our destination node.

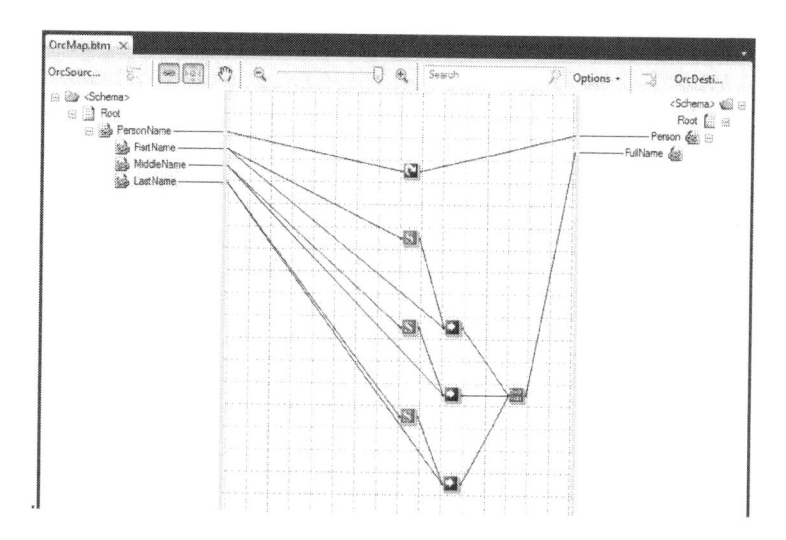

Figure 54: Map example

After developing all our schemas and maps, we can start our orchestration development. To do so, right-click your project in the Solution Explorer and click **Add New Item**. In the new item selection screen, select **Orchestration**. BizTalk will then open the Orchestration Editor.

Once the Editor opens, drag the receive shape and drop it into the designer as shown in Figure 55. It's a best practice to rename to shapes to names that will suggest their function and execution.

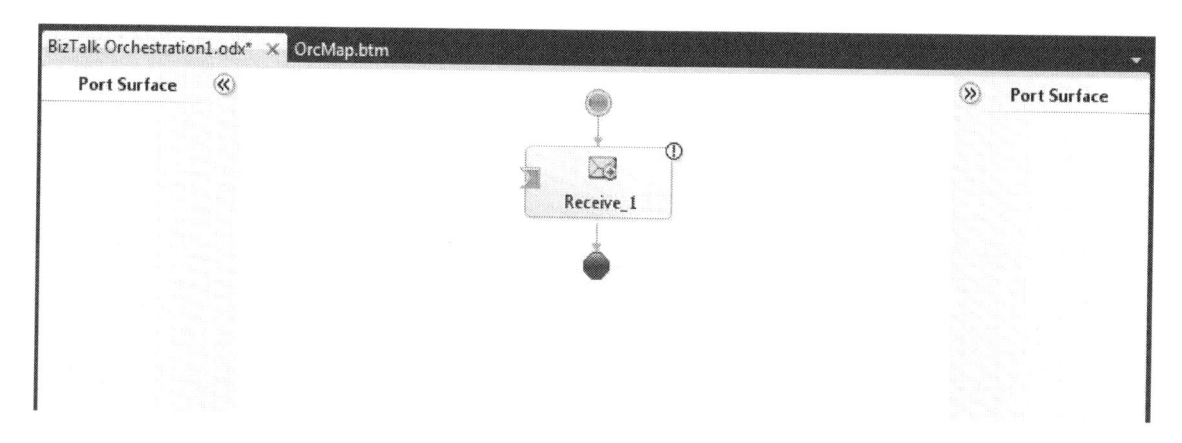

Figure 55: Add receive shape

Next, add the transformation shape to the designer, and add the send shape. This will allow you to set up a process in which a message is received, transformed using a map, and sent to a location using the send shape. As you can see in this very simple example, however, orchestrations can become complicated when you start adding intelligence to them. Once you add the three shapes, you should have an orchestration as shown in Figure 56.

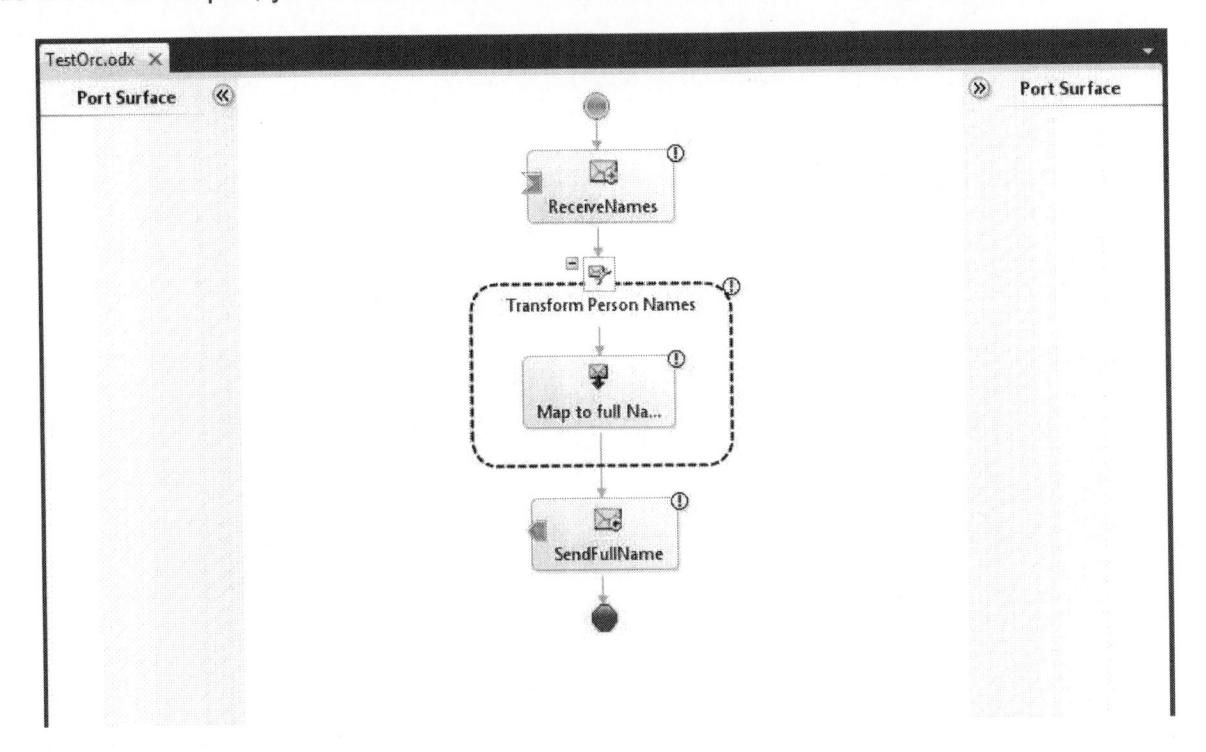

Figure 56: Example orchestration

After designing our orchestration, it's now time to configure it, setting up the messages and ports it will use. Let's start with the messages. Just as we have one source schema and one destination schema, we are going to have two messages as well—one based in the source schema, and another based on the destination schema. To create a new message, right-click the **Message** folder in the Orchestration View panel and select **New Message**.

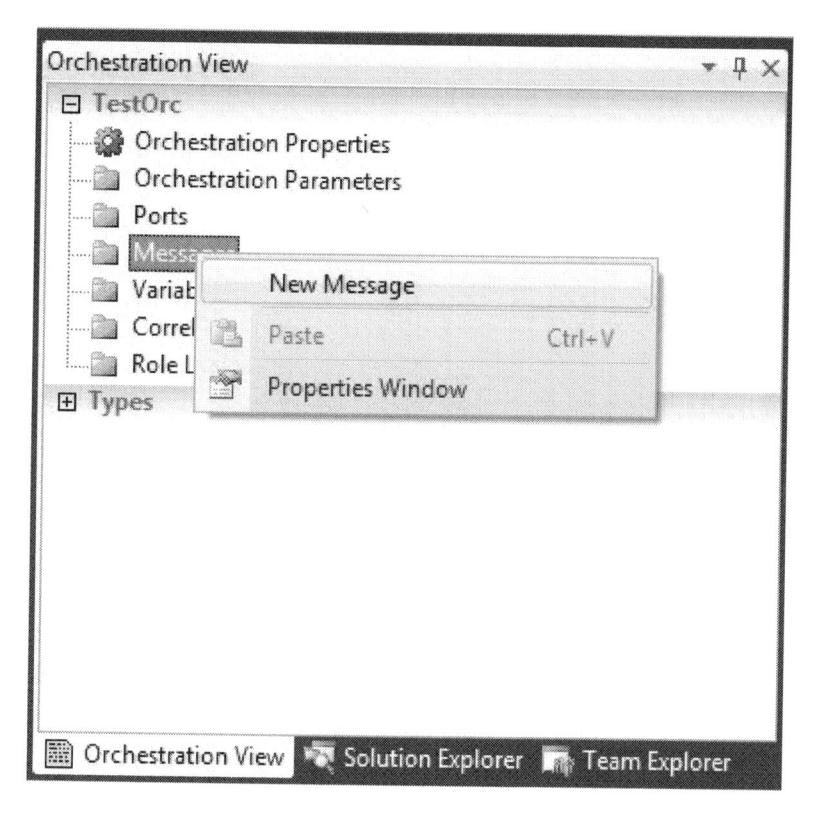

Figure 57: New Messages

BizTalk will open the New Message properties in the Properties window. Give the message a name, and in the **Message Type** property, select the schema it should be based on, as illustrated in Figure 58.

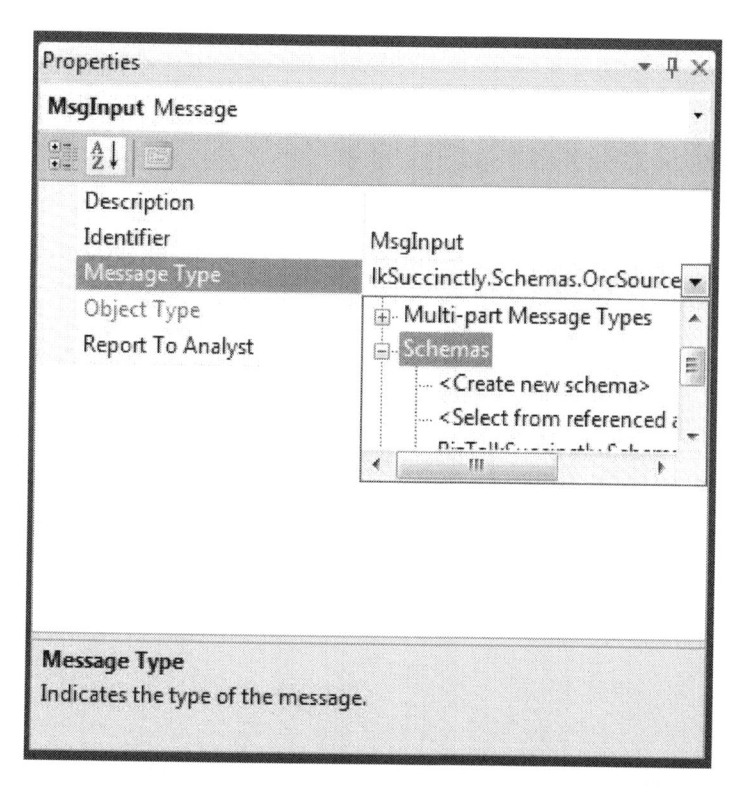

Figure 58: Configure New Messages

In this example we are going to create two messages: one called MsgInput, for the Source Schema message type, and another one called MsgOutput, for the Destination Schema message type. When you finish creating and configuring both, your message folder should have the messages shown in Figure 59.

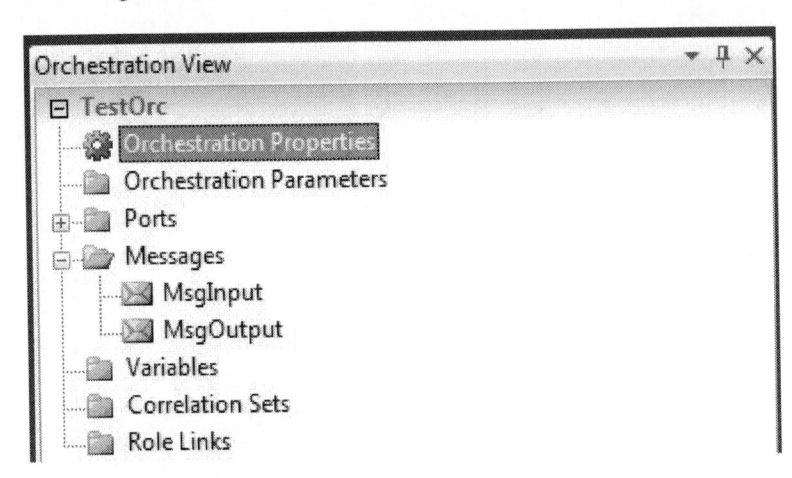

Figure 59: Messages created

After creating the messages, it's time to tell our receive/send shapes which message type they should be expecting when a document arrives to one of their ports. In this example, we have one receive shape and one send shape. To start with the receive shape, click it in the designer and, in the Properties window, configure the **Message** property to **MsgInput**. Set the **Send Shape** property to **MsgOutput**.

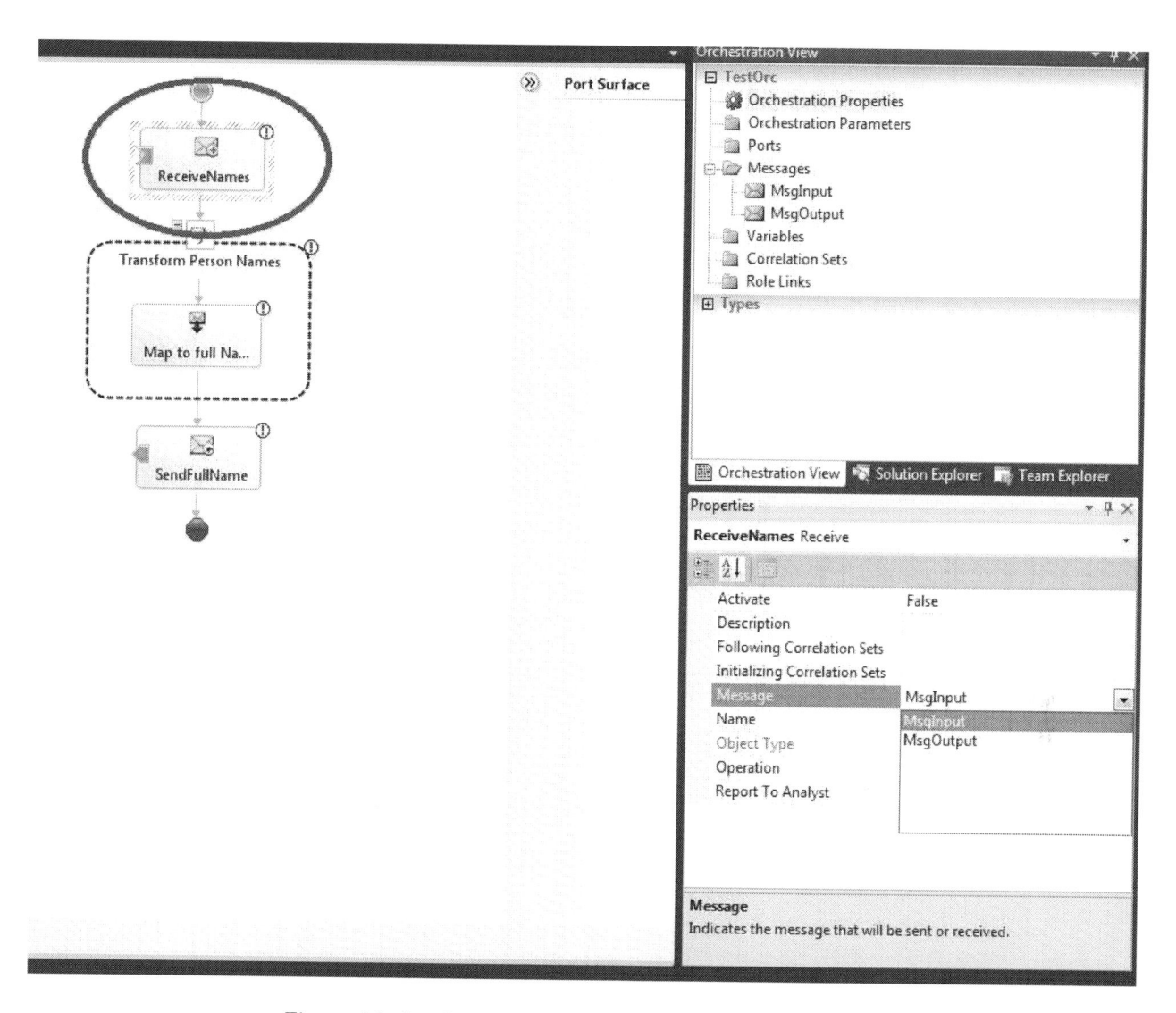

Figure 60: Configure Receive/Send shape message

Now, let's set up our transformation shape. Double-click it, and the Transform Configuration window will appear. Figure 61 shows you this screen.

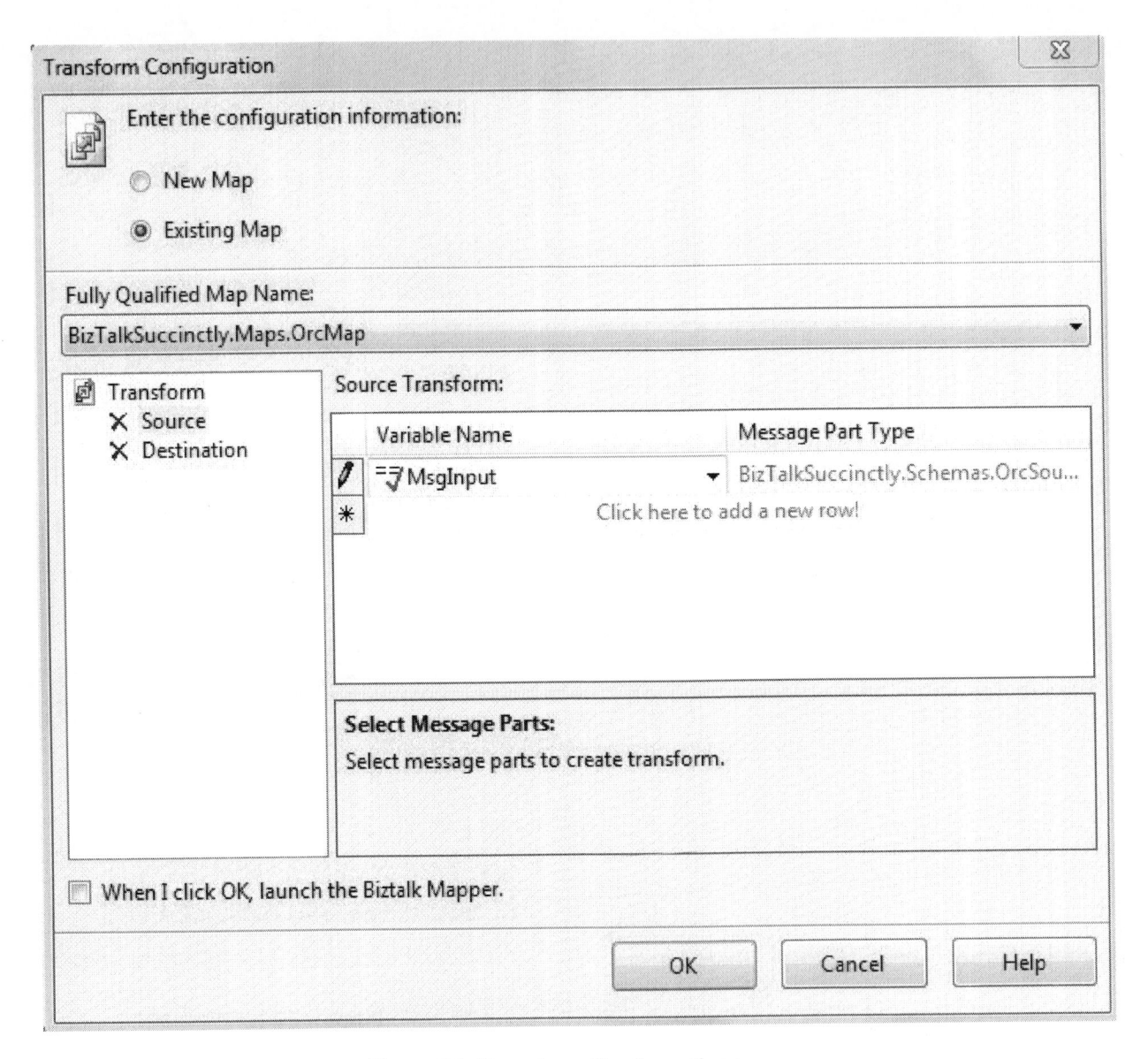

Figure 61: Transform Configurations

In this configuration screen, you are going to tell the orchestration how it should transform the MsgInput when it arrives. Choose the **Existing Map** radio button on top of the screen, so that we can select our created map. Next, select our map in the **Fully Qualified Map Name** property. Last, we need to tell the transform shape which is the input message and which is the output message. Select our already created messages in the respective **Variable Name** combo box.

As you can see, we haven't defined any receive or send ports, just the shapes. Note that these are just logical ports, not physical ports; those are going to be configured later in the BizTalk Server Administrator.

To configure these logical ports in the orchestration, you need to drag and drop the port shape to the **Port Surface** lane of the the orchestration designer. There are two Port Surfaces, one for receive ports on the left, and another for send ports on the right of the designer. Figure 62 shows you the receive ports lane.

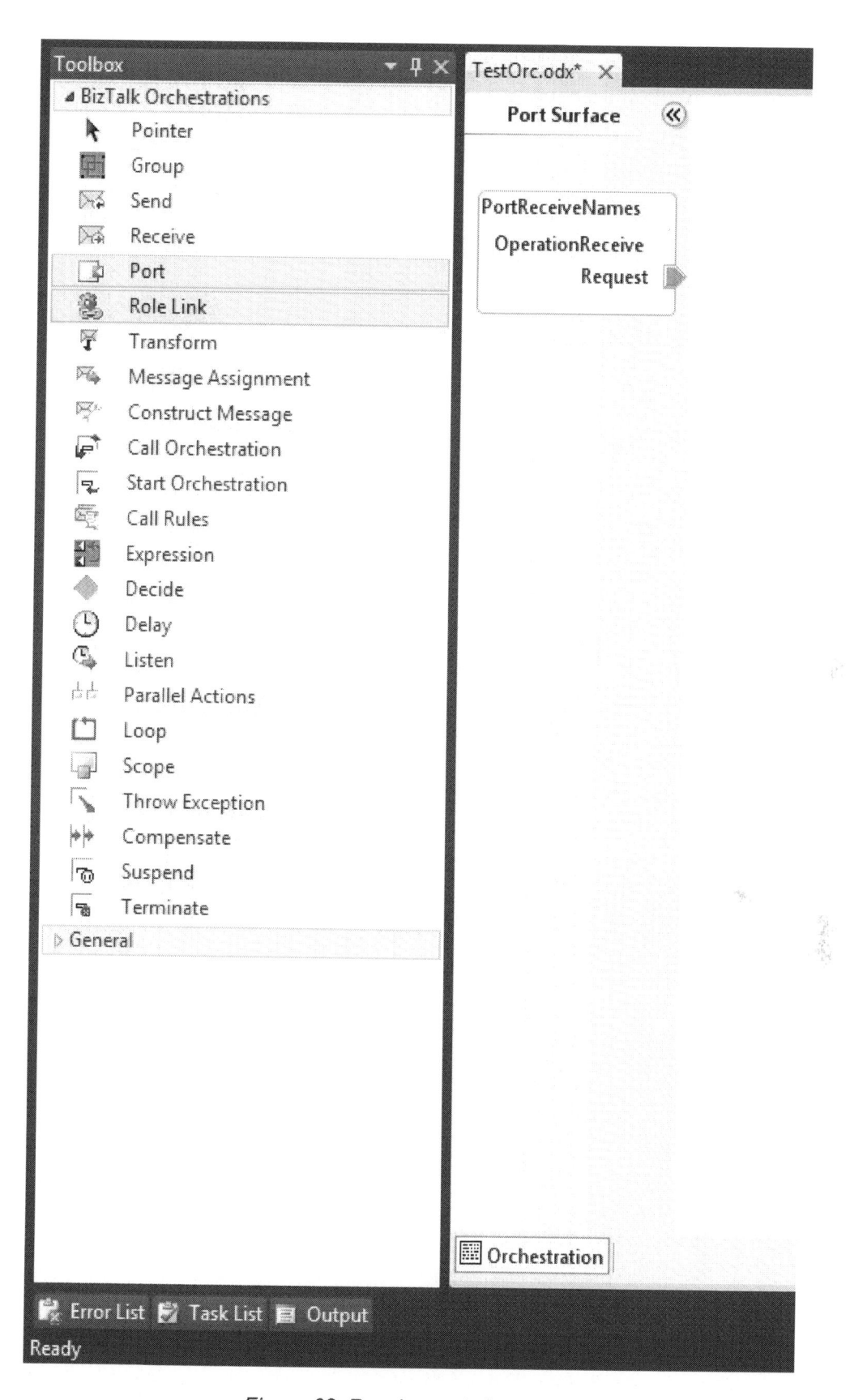

Figure 62: Receive ports lane

Now let's add the first port to the orchestration—the receive port. To do so, drag and drop it to the port surface lane on the left. Once you drop it, BizTalk will launch the Port Configuration Wizard, as you can see in Figure 63.

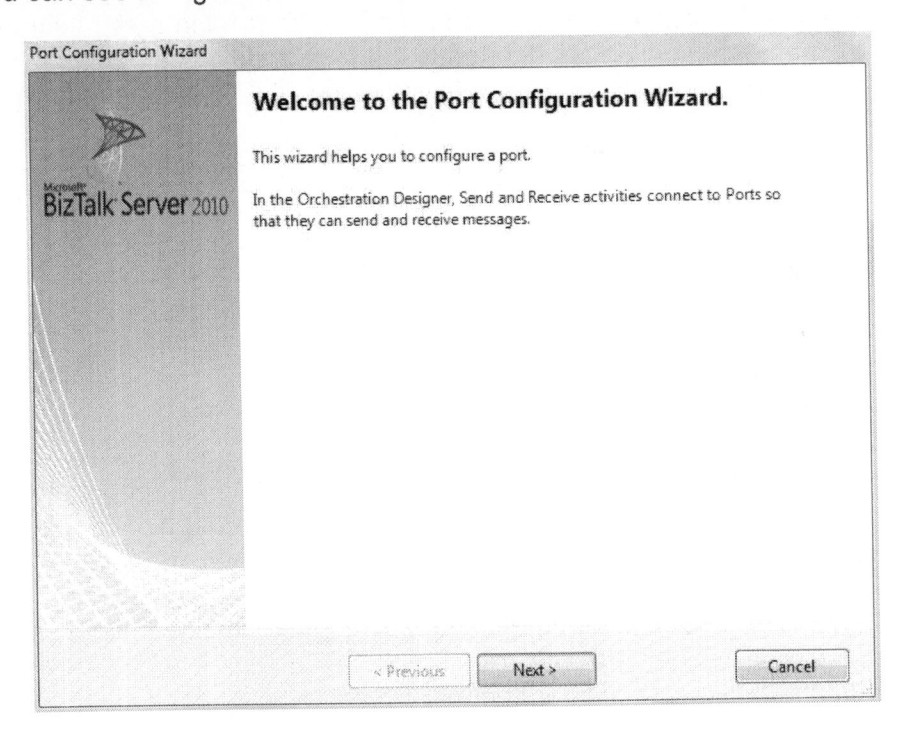

Figure 63: Port configuration Wizard

The first step in this wizard is naming the port.

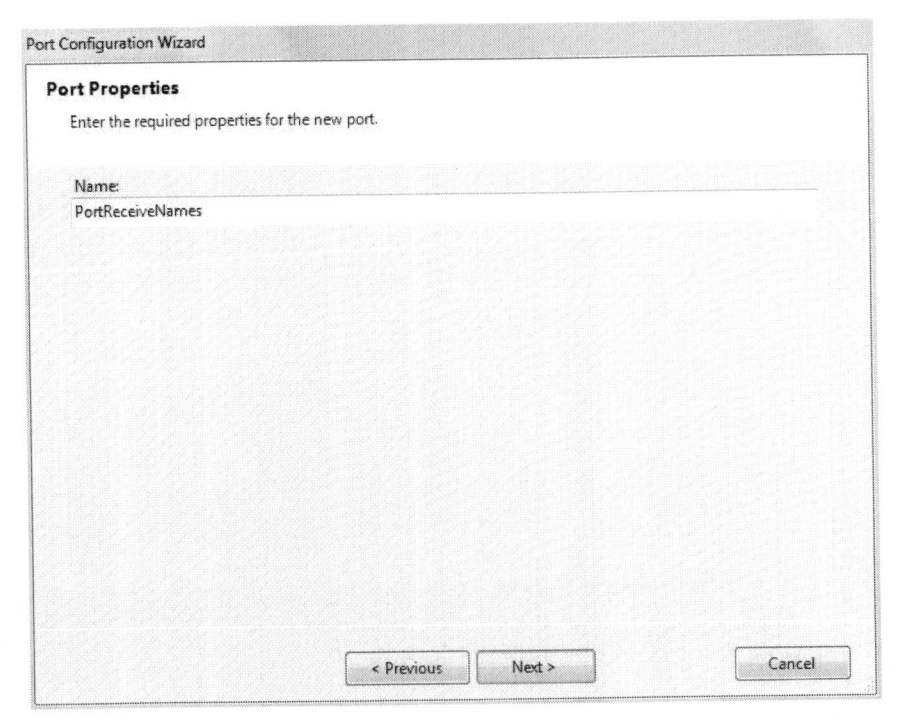

Figure 64: Port configuration Wizard—Name

Once you click on **Next**, the wizard will take you to one of the most important screens in the Port Configuration Wizard, where you set up the Port Type, which defines the direction of your port (one or two way) and the access restrictions. Figure 65 shows this Port Configuration screen.

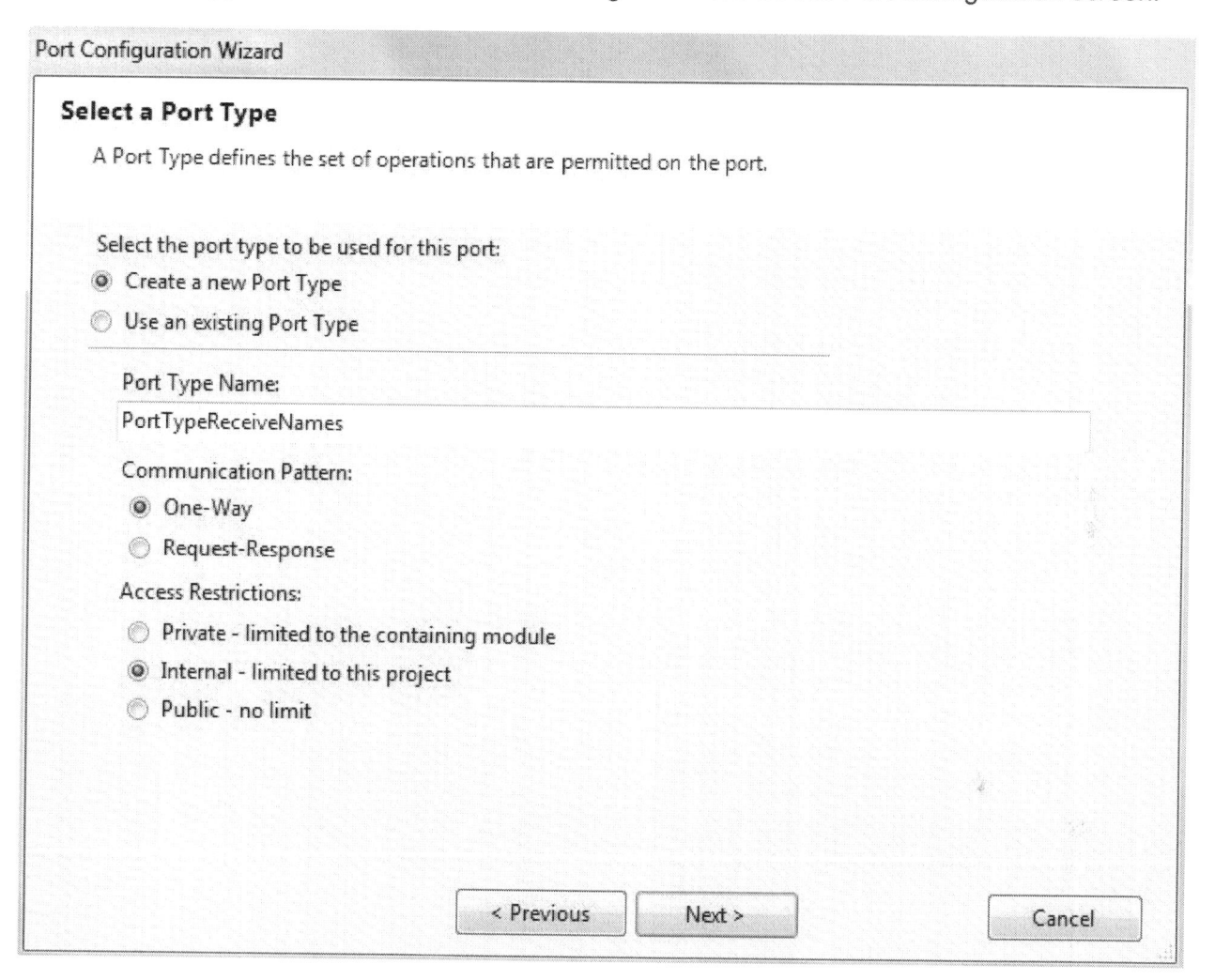

Figure 65: Configure Port Type

The first configuration item lets you choose between creating a new port type and using an existing one. For our example, select **Create a new Port Type**.

Next, give your port type a name and select **One-Way** as the Communication Pattern. This one-way option defines that your port will only receive or send messages. We will choose this one because we are going to transform our received message, and only after that send it, so we need to create two distinct ports—one to receive, and another to send. However, if you wanted to receive and send to a partner without any transformation, or even communicate with a web service in which you send a request and receive a response, you could use the Request-Response pattern.

The available access restriction lets you define who can use this port type: only this module (Private), only the artifacts allowed to use port types within this project (Internal), or everyone (Public). Let's choose the Internal option for our example, as this will be a single project port type. Although we will be choosing the internal options, as you can see, there are three types of access restrictions:

- **Private**—This port type can be used only within this orchestration
- **Internal**—This port type can be used across different orchestrations within this project
- **Public**—This port type can be used by anyone in any project

After defining your port type, select **Next** to open the Port Binding screen of the Configuration Wizard. As you can see, you haven't yet defined whether this is a receive or a send port; this configuration is set in this screen. Now, as we are creating a receive port, lets choose **I'll always be receiving messages on this port** under **Port direction of communication**. Under **Port binding**, choose **Specify later**, as we are binding the ports with the BizTalk Administrator later. Click **Next**.

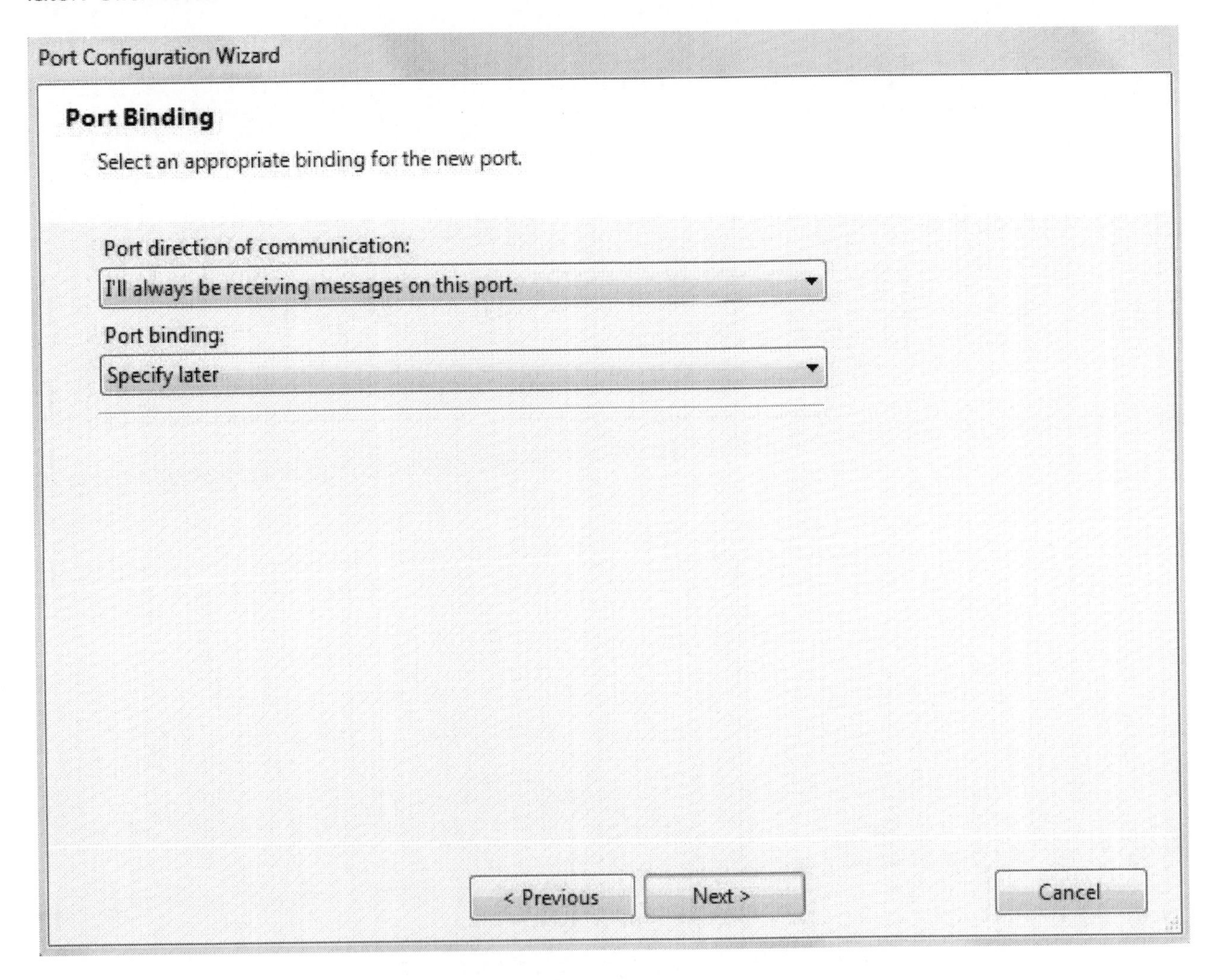

Figure 66: Configure receive port type

Port Binding is the configuration information that determines where and how a message will be sent or received. Depending on its type, a port binding might refer to physical locations, pipelines, or other orchestrations. There are three types of port bindings for receive messages:

- **Specify Now**—Allows you to specify at design time what pipeline you want to use and the location you want to communicate with. It is also called "Binding at Design Time."
- **Specify Later**—If you do not have all of the information you need to specify a physical location, you can select the Specify Later port binding option in the Orchestration Designer, and you only need to specify the port type that describes the port. Also called "Binding at Deployment Time."
- **Direct**—Your orchestration can communicate directly with another orchestration by using direct binding. In this case, the message is processed internally by the engine, and no external transport of the message takes place.

There is one last port binding type, which is restricted to send messages:

- **Dynamic**—If you will not know the location of a communication until run time, you can use dynamic binding for a send port. The location might, for example, be determined from a property on an incoming message.

When the wizard is complete, BizTalk will take you back to the orchestration designer. Now it's time to link this recently created receive port to our receive shape. This is how you tell the orchestration that those receive messages will arrive from this port and port type.

Figure 67 shows you how your orchestration should look at this point:

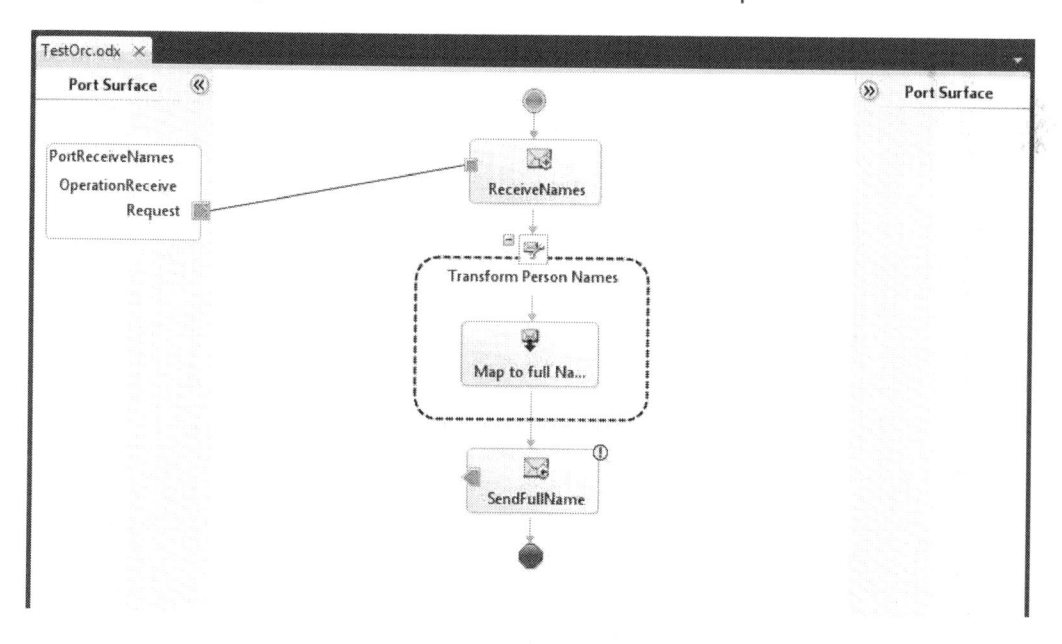

Figure 67: Link the port to the receive shape

Now, repeat this process for the send port. Drag and drop the port shape to the Port Surface on the right of the designer, and configure your port using the Port Creation Wizard, giving attention to the step in which you define if your port is a receive or send port. Figure 68 illustrates the Port Binding step.

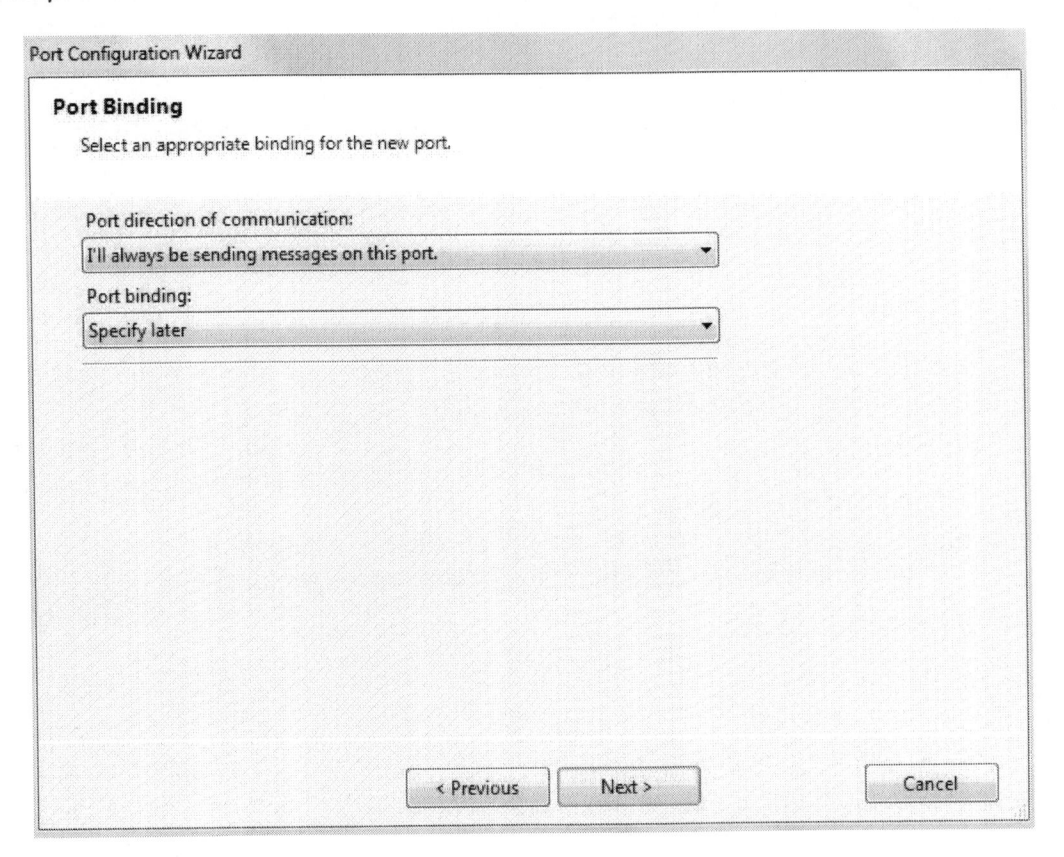

Figure 68: Configure send port

To finish the design of our orchestration, link the recently created send port to the send shape, and your orchestration should look like Figure 69.

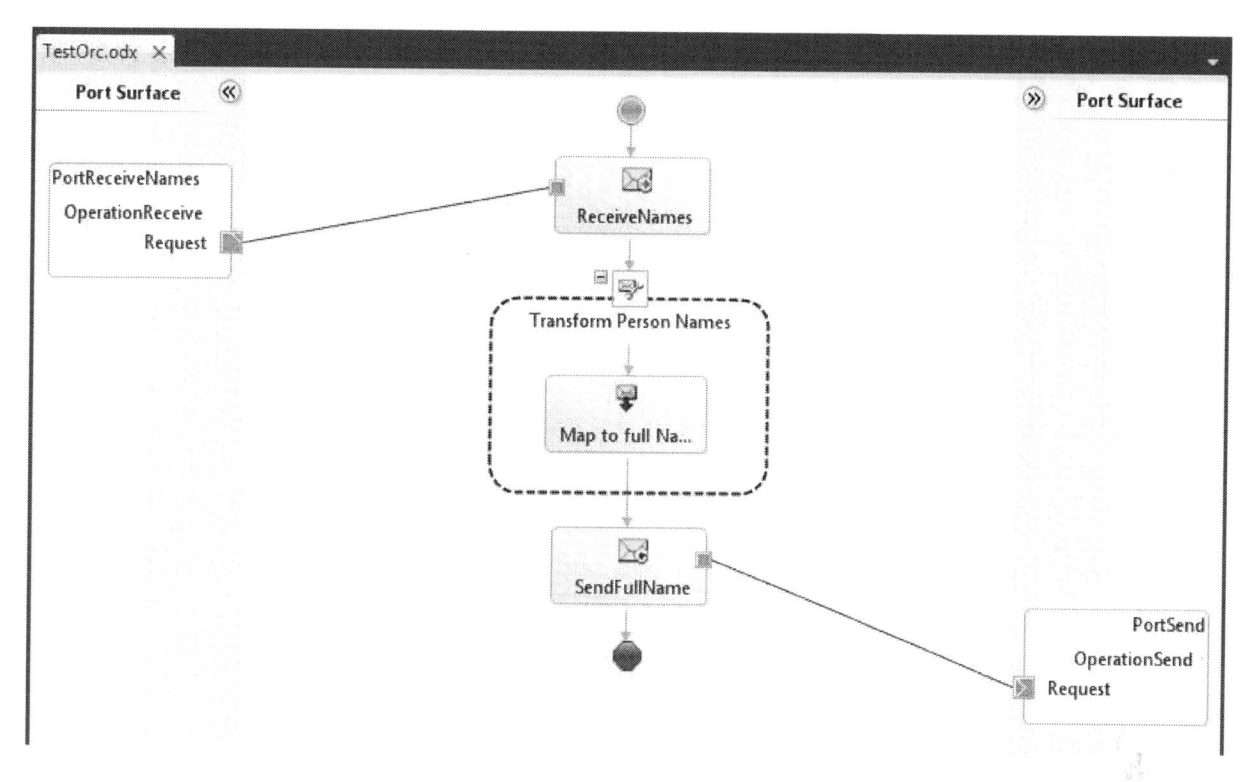

Figure 69: Final orchestration examples

Even though it might look like it's complete, you still need to make several configurations before compiling and deploying your application to the BizTalk Server. The first mandatory step is to set an active receive shape, as BizTalk requires that at least one receive shape is listening to message arrival in our orchestration. This is a common error for those new to BizTalk Server. Figure 70 shows you the error message when you try to compile your application without an active receive shape.

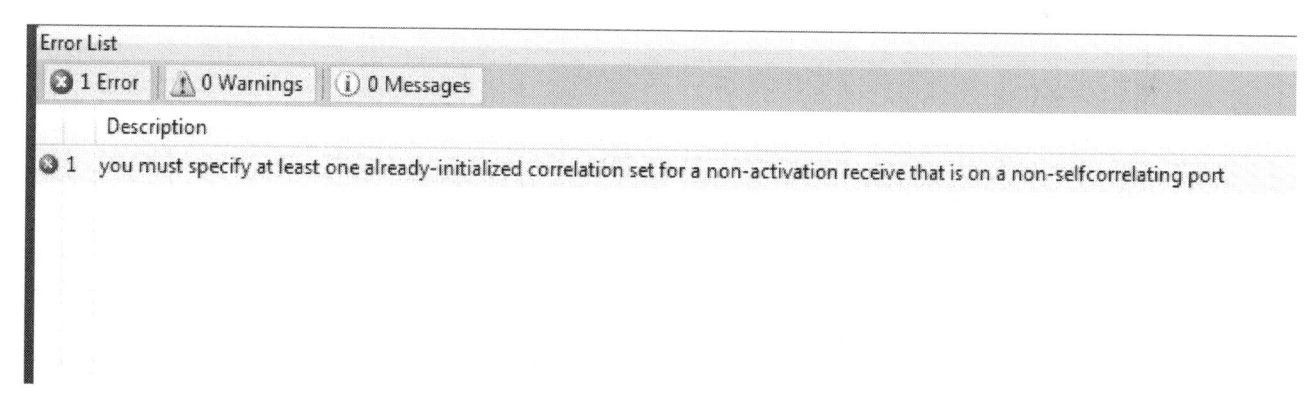

Figure 70: Error when there is no active receive shape

To avoid this problem, you should select the receive shape you want to activate, and in the Properties window for your receive shape, set the **Activate** property to **True**.

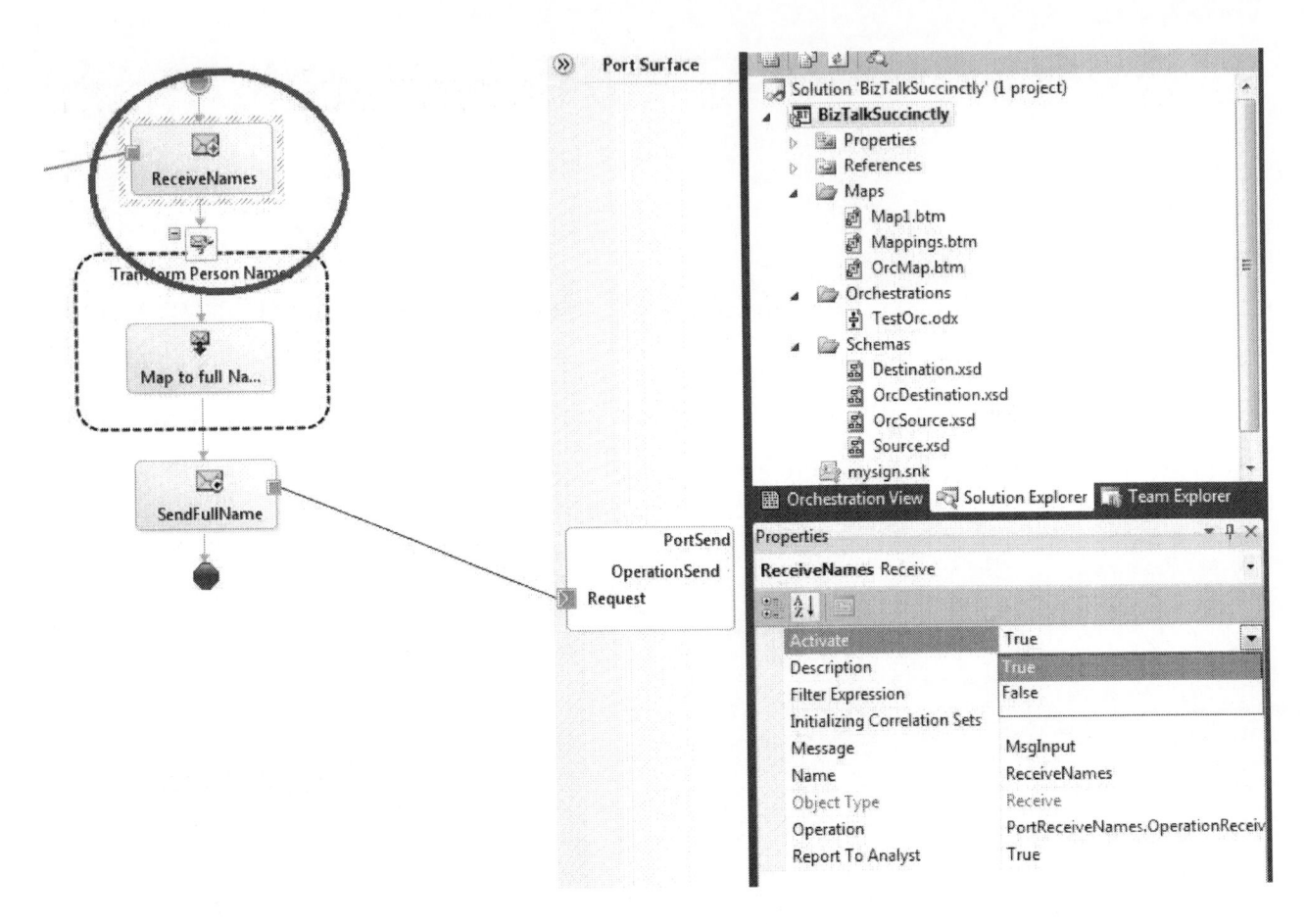

Figure 71: Activate receive shape

Now your application is ready to be compiled and deployed to the BizTalk Server. The next chapter will show you how.

Chapter 9 Deploy to the Server using Visual Studio

Until now we have been talking about development, creating schemas and transforming them using maps, and building workflows for business processes using orchestrations, but our project isn't working in production yet. To do so, we need to deploy it to the server so that BizTalk can create a running application, and so that we can create all the physical ports for our application.

As I have already mentioned, building a project in Visual Studio and event-defining ports in orchestrations is a logical operation, as you can use the same project for multiple companies and will only need to deploy it to their servers and configure the physical artifacts on the application.

Deployment

Deploying your application is a very fast and easy step. Just right-click your project in the Solution Explorer and select the **Properties** option to configure the application name, deployment database, and the server you want to deploy to.

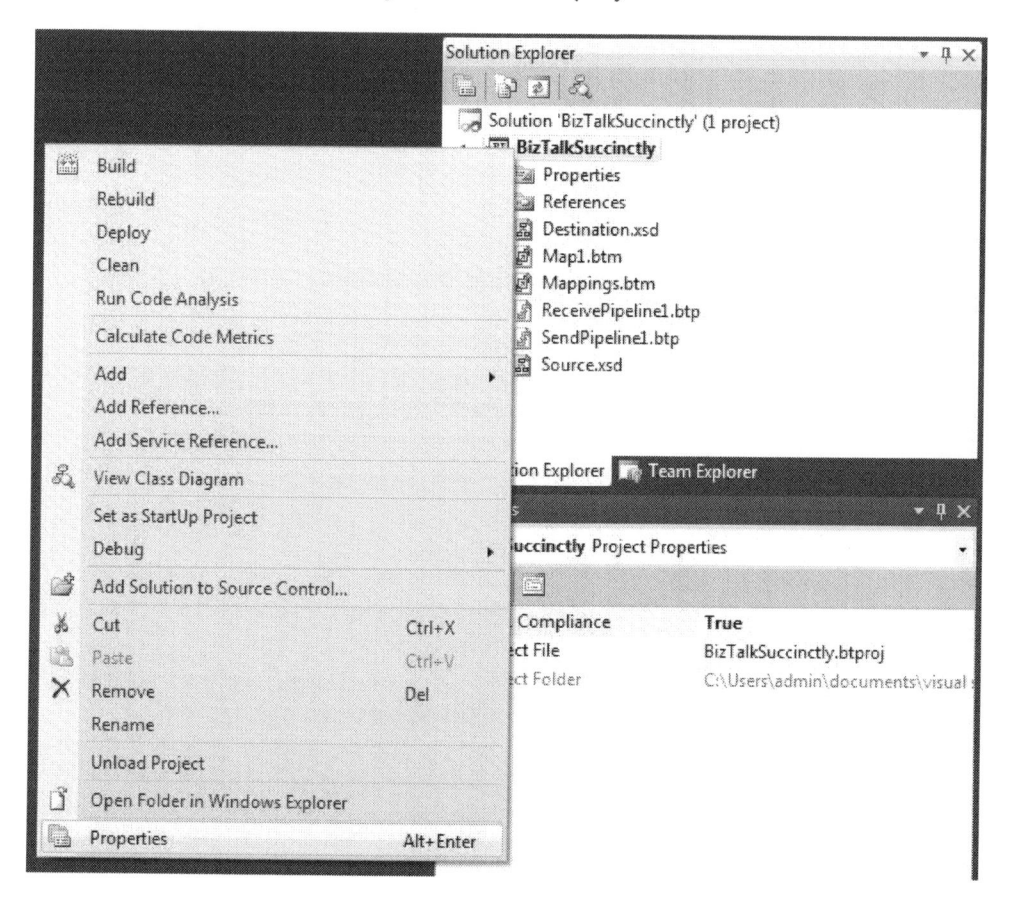

Figure 72: Project properties

When the Properties window opens, go to the **Deployment** tab and give your application a name (if not set, it will be deployed to Application 1), and make sure that the Configuration Database and Server are configured according to your needs. If you are using BizTalk Developer installed with default settings, you should see something like Figure 73:

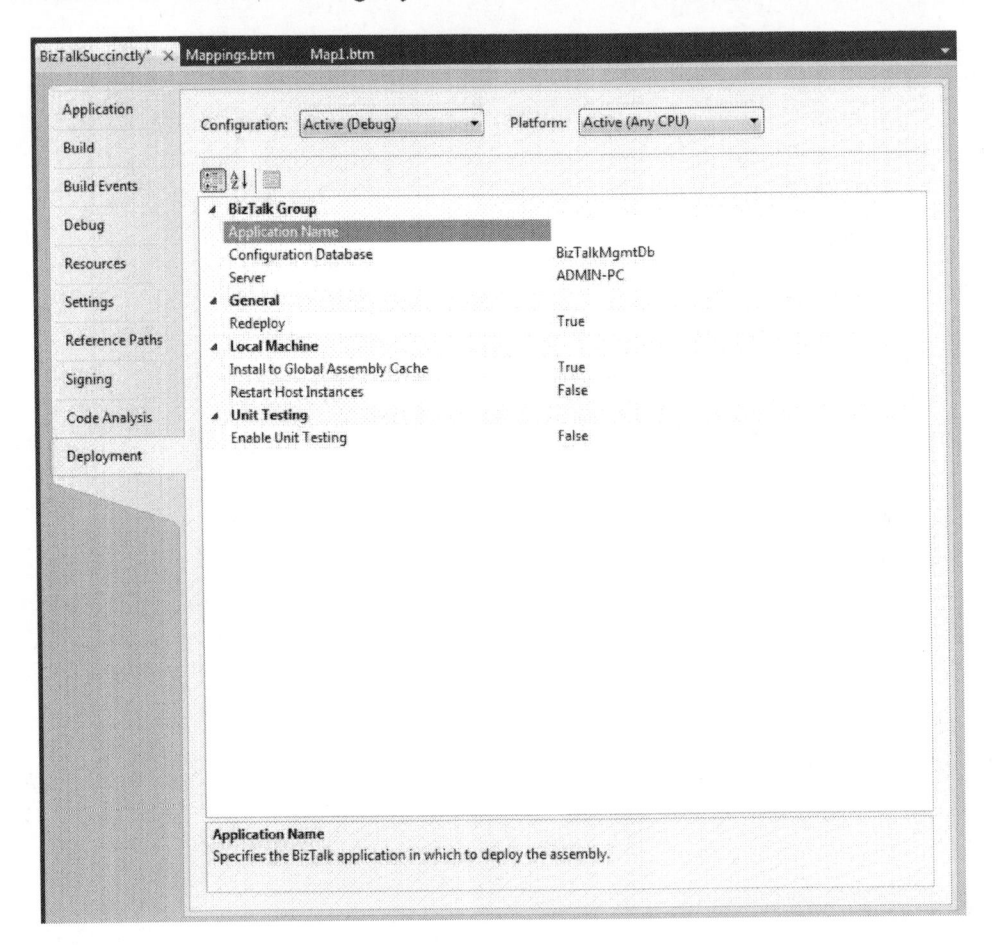

Figure 73: Configure application name

The second setting you need to configure is the signing of the project. BizTalk uses strong names for DLLs, so a strong name key file is required. Go to the **Signing** tab and use an existing one if you have it, or create a simple one by selecting the **Sign the assembly** checkbox and the **New** option in the list box.

Because all BizTalk Assemblies need to be installed or registered in the Global Assembly Cache (GAC), you need to sign them with a strong name key. An example can be seen in the Figure 74.

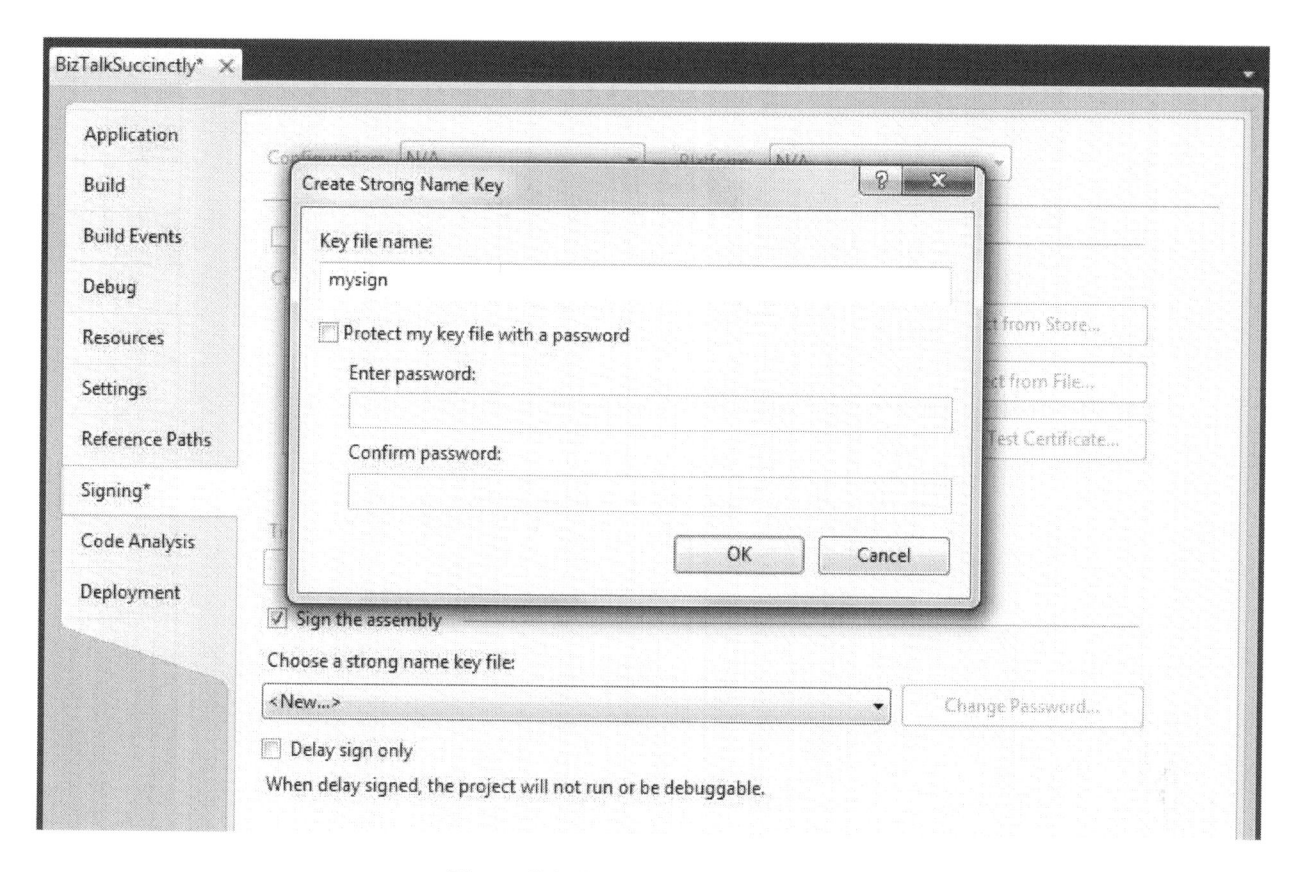

Figure 74: Signing the project

After naming the application and setting a signature, save your changes, right-click your project in the Solution Explorer, and select **Deploy**. Please make sure you are running Visual Studio with elevated privileges.

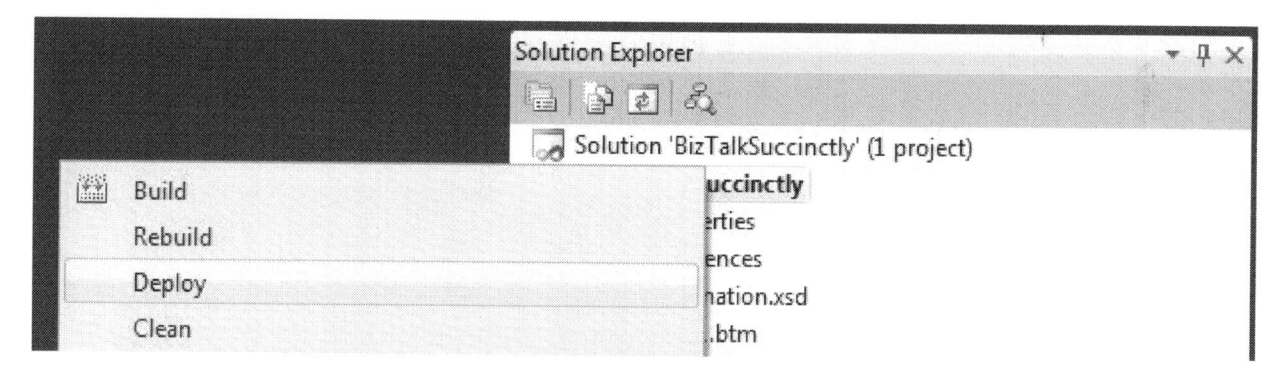

Figure 75: Deploy the project

Once the deployment is complete, the output windows will show you a success message, or an error message if anything went wrong. In our case, we had a success message, as you can see in Figure 76.

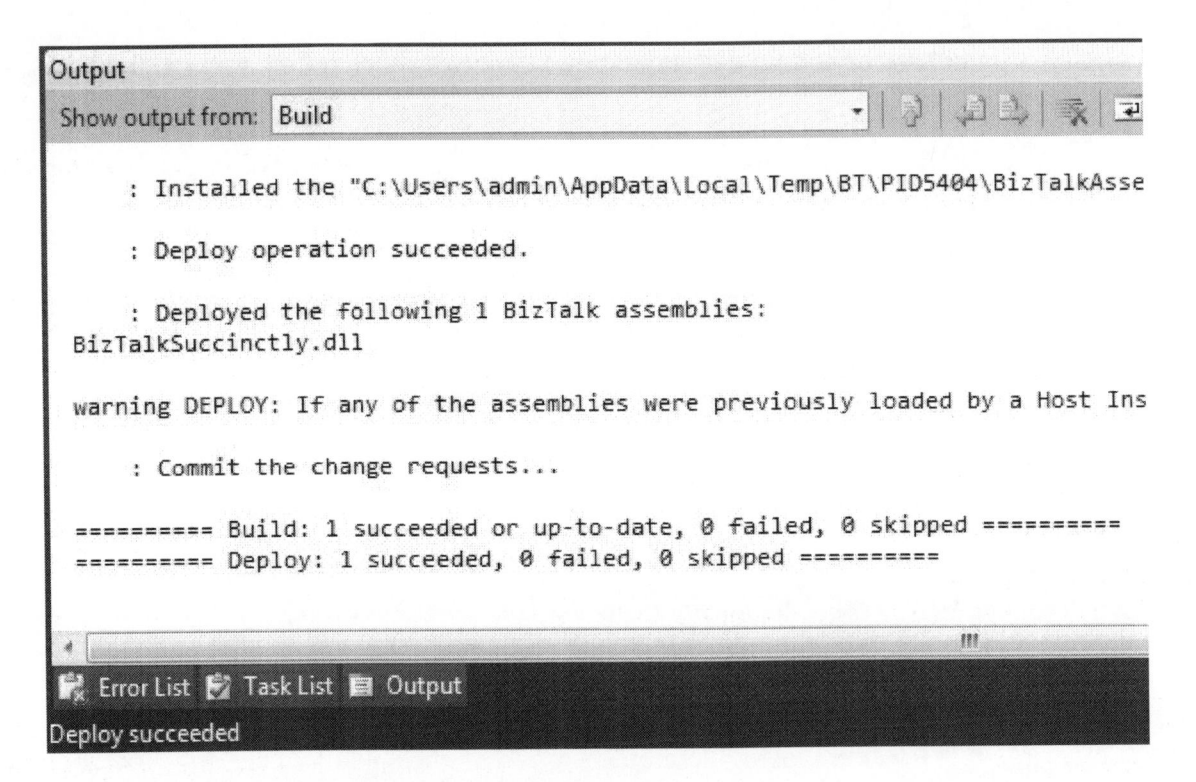

```
: Installed the "C:\Users\admin\AppData\Local\Temp\BT\PID5404\BizTalkAsse

: Deploy operation succeeded.

: Deployed the following 1 BizTalk assemblies:
BizTalkSuccinctly.dll

warning DEPLOY: If any of the assemblies were previously loaded by a Host Ins

: Commit the change requests...

========== Build: 1 succeeded or up-to-date, 0 failed, 0 skipped ==========
========== Deploy: 1 succeeded, 0 failed, 0 skipped ==========
```

Figure 76: Successful Deployments

You can now open BizTalk Server Administrator, and you will see your application in the application list. The next steps are configuring and testing the application.

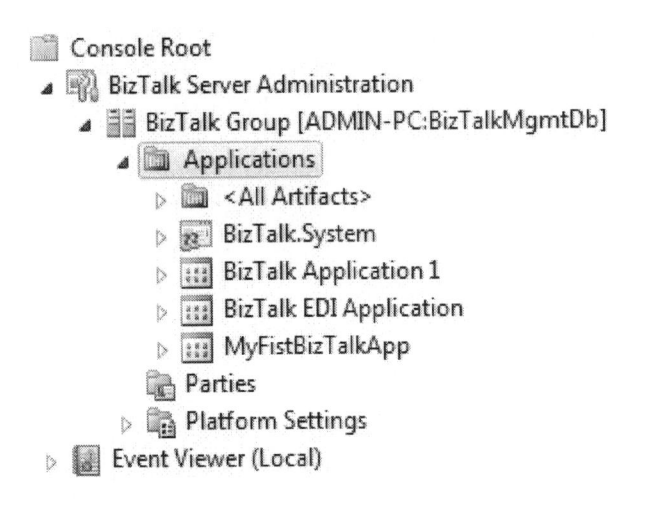

- Console Root
  - BizTalk Server Administration
    - BizTalk Group [ADMIN-PC:BizTalkMgmtDb]
      - Applications
        - <All Artifacts>
        - BizTalk.System
        - BizTalk Application 1
        - BizTalk EDI Application
        - MyFistBizTalkApp
      - Parties
      - Platform Settings
  - Event Viewer (Local)

Figure 77: Applications in BTS Administrator

Chapter 10 Configuring the BizTalk Administrator

To configure our application, we are going to use BizTalk Server Administrator. I won't go into too much detail on this, as it would take an entire book just to explain how to use all the administration tasks, and how can they affect your application's performance. Instead I will cover only the configurations needed to get our small application running.

To open the BizTalk Server Administration Console, take the following steps:

1. Click **Start**.
2. Select **Programs**.
3. Select **Microsoft BizTalk Server 2010**.
4. Select **BizTalk Server Administration**.

On the left side of the Administrator, you have a tree view that allows you to navigate between these console options and components. Once you open the tree, you will find the Applications node containing our deployed applications. As you can see, our MyFirstBizTalkApp is available as a child of the Applications node. If you expand it, you will find all elements of this application organized into folders, which contain all artifacts created in the BizTalk developer environment (schemas, maps, orchestrations, ports, and any other resources).

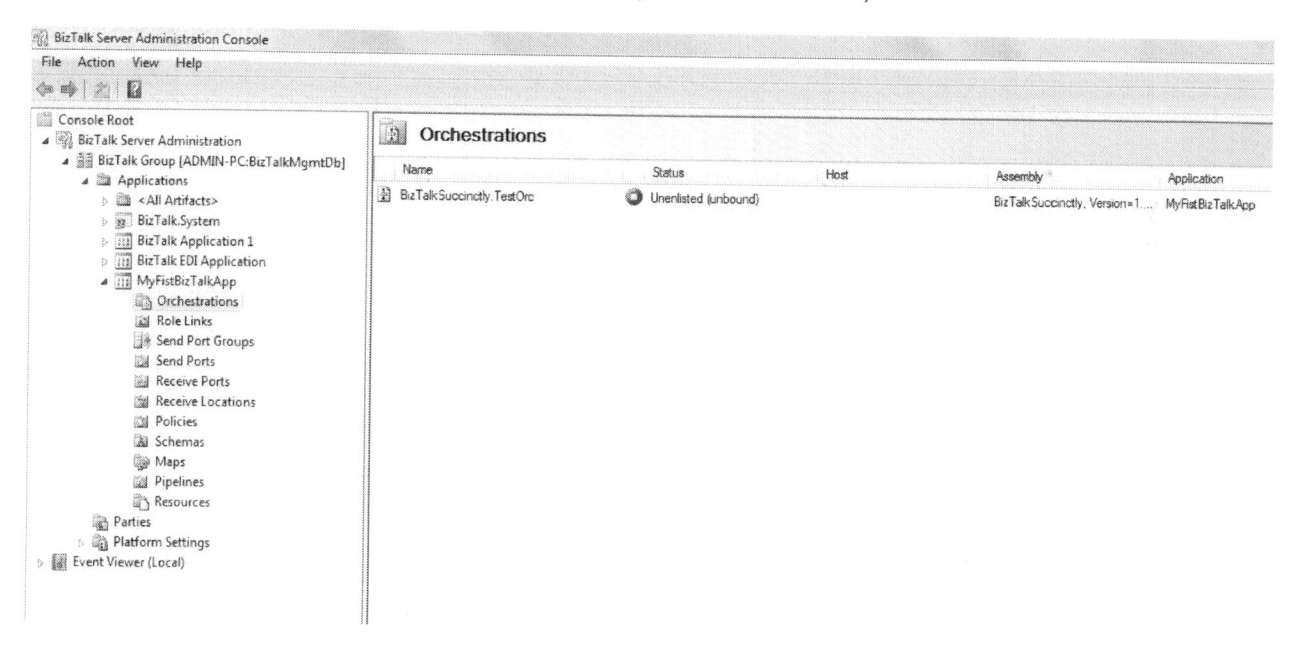

Figure 78: First view of the BizTalk Administrator

In our example from Chapter 8, we developed a simple application with one receive port, one send port, and a transformation. In order to test it, we need to manually bind a physical location for the receive messages and a physical location for the send messages, specify which process (host instance) they will running, and then bind these ports to those existing in our orchestration.

In order to make our application work, we need to complete the following steps:

1. Configure the receive port and location.
2. Configure the send port and location.
3. Configure the orchestration.
4. Start the application.
5. Test the application.

Configure the receive port

Our first step is configuring the receive port. Select the **Receive Ports** option in the Application Node in the tree view window on the left. The Receive Ports folder will open. To create a new receive port, right-click in the center of the screen, select **New**, and then select **One-Way Receive Port**, as you can see in Figure 79.

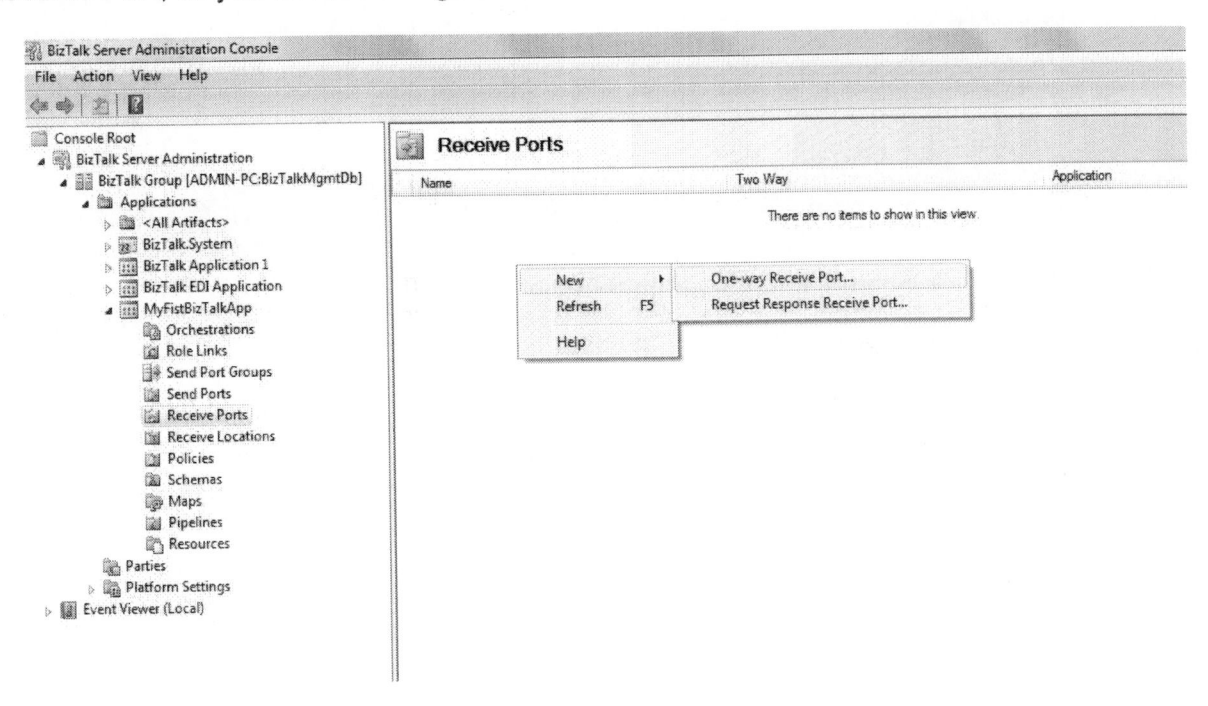

Figure 79: Create a new receive port

BizTalk Administrator will start a wizard that will assist you with the configuration. As you can see in Figure 80, you need to set up a receive port name and the authentication level. For our example, select **No authentication**, as we won't need any to handle our receive messages.

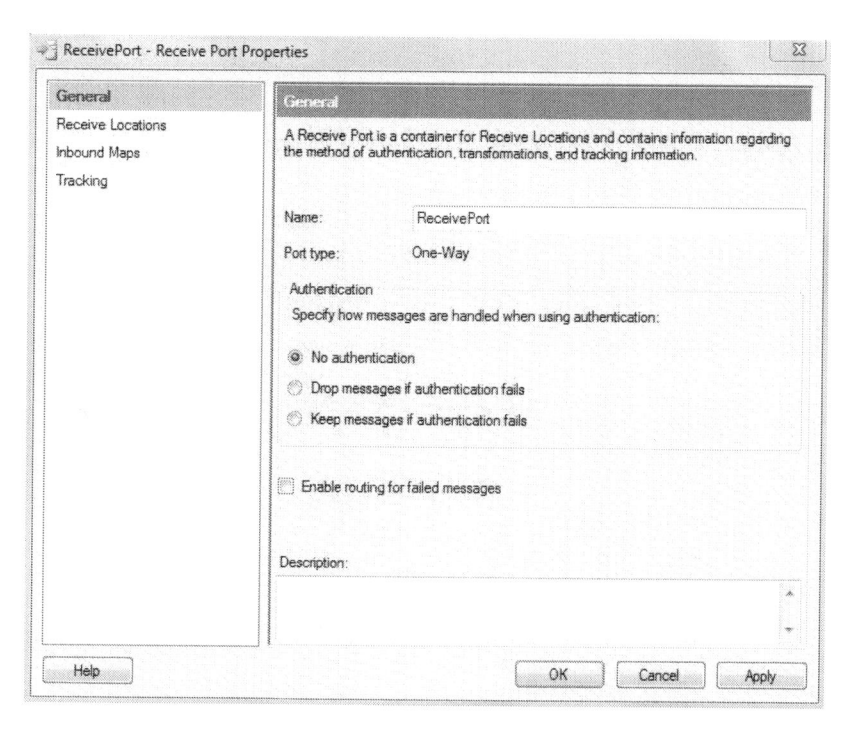

Figure 80: Configure receive port

Next, click **Receive Locations** in the left pane of the wizard screen. This where we are going to tell BizTalk to use a specific physical location as our message receiving location. Click **New...** in the Receive Locations window.

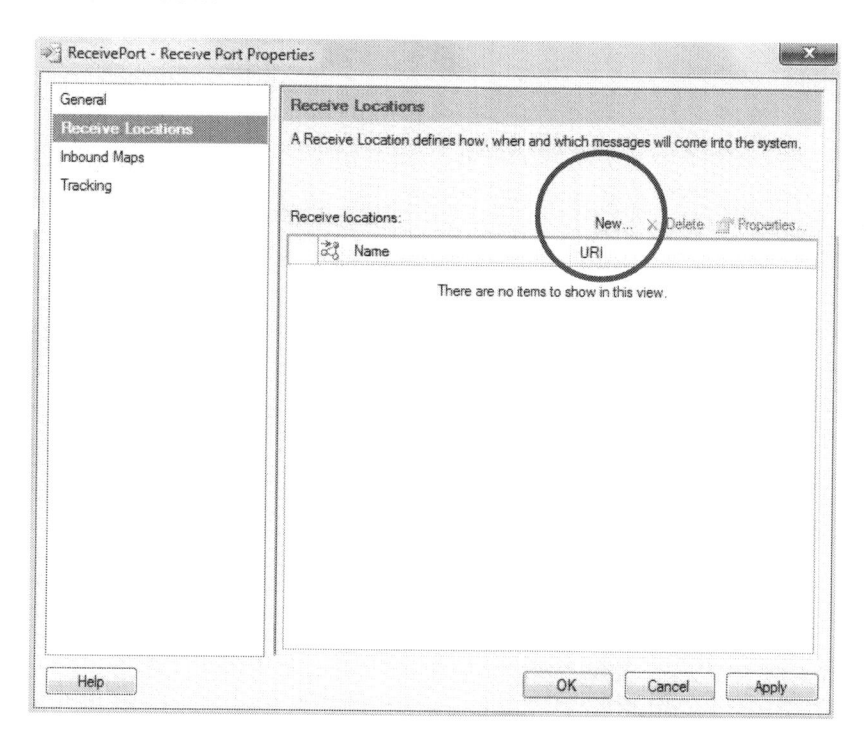

Figure 81: Create a new receive location

This will open a new Receive Locations window, in which you select the adapter you need to use from one of the following out-of-the-box options:

- FILE
- FTP
- HTTP
- MQSeries
- MSMQ
- POP3
- SOAP
- SQL
- WCF
- Windows SharePoint Services

As you can see, BizTalk allows for many adapters. An adapter is a software component that enables you to easily send messages out of or receive messages into BizTalk Server with a delivery mechanism that conforms to a commonly recognized standard, such as SMTP, POP3, FTP, or Microsoft Message Queuing (MSMQ). As Microsoft BizTalk Server has evolved, the need for adapters that quickly enable connectivity with commonly used applications and technologies has increased. For our example, we will use the FILE transport type.

Select **FILE** in the **Type** combo box, and select the **Receive handler** for this port, which by default will be **BizTalk Server Application**. Don't forget to select **XMLReceive** in the **Receive pipeline** field; this way the message will be disassembled and the subscribers can be identified. Otherwise, if you choose the PassThruReceive pipeline, BizTalk will raise an error saying that no subscribers were identified.

Now click **Configure** so that you can define the URI for your location.

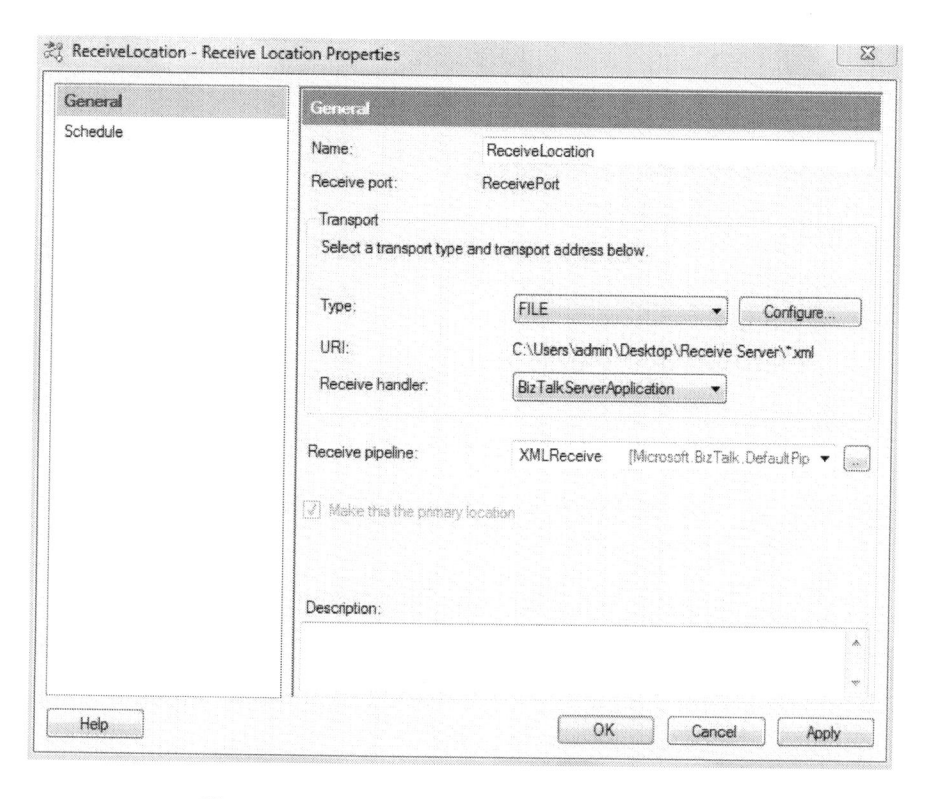

Figure 82: Receive Location Properties

Next, you will be prompted with a FILE Transport Properties window in which you can set the **Receive folder** path. This will be our simulating **Receive Server**. Since we will be dealing with XML files as input, select the file mask *.xml so that only xml files will be processed.

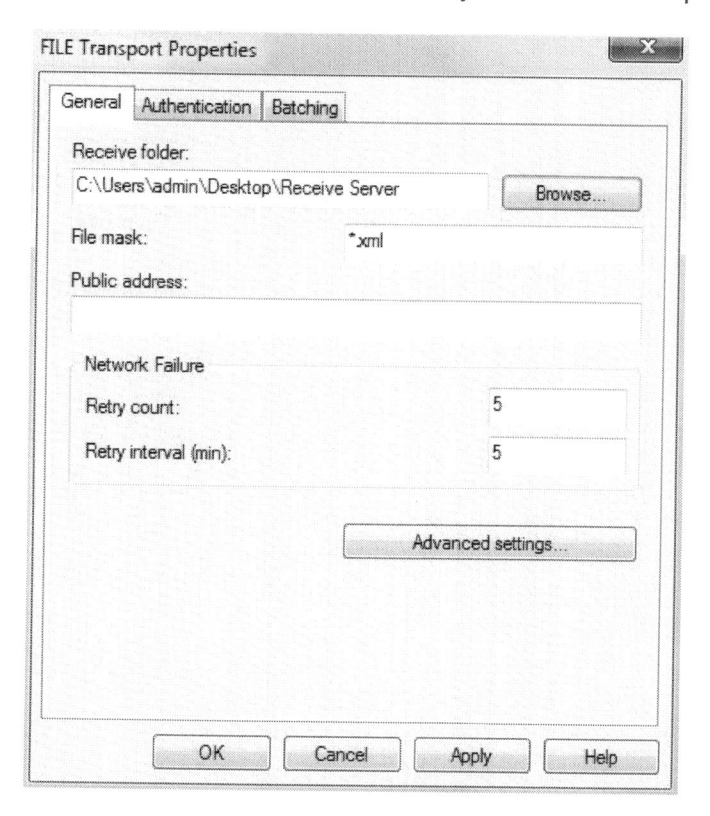

Figure 83: Configure receive folder

Click **OK** in the FILE Transport Properties window, and continue to click **OK** for all open windows for this Receive Port configuration. When you are done, you will see a new object inside the Receive Ports folder, which is your recently created port.

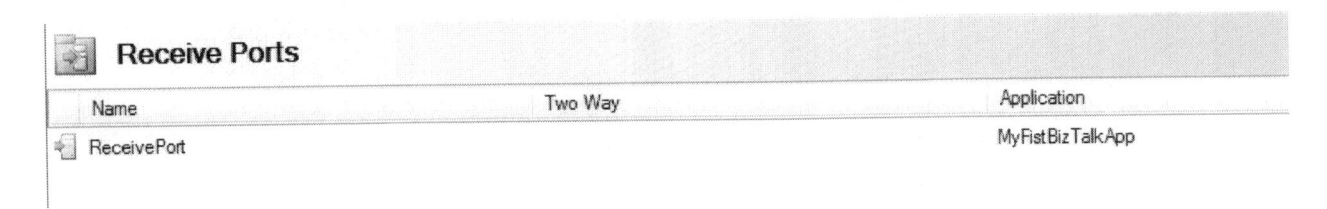

Figure 84: Created receive port

Now you'll do the same for the send port—the only difference is the pipeline you will use. Since we are expecting our result message format and the BizTalk internal message format to be XML, you don't need any special processing, so you can use the **PassThruSend** pipeline. Once you create the send port, you should see it appear in the Send Port folder. The only difference will be a red symbol in the Status field port, which indicates that this port is stopped.

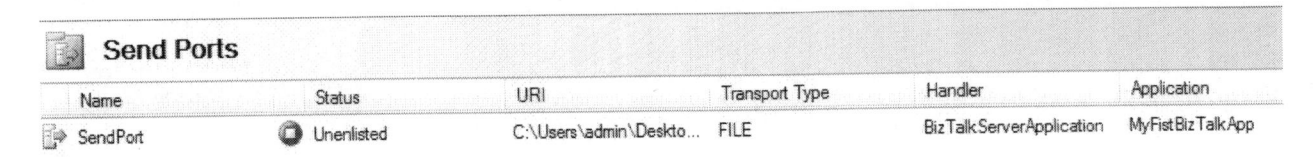

Figure 85: Unlisted ports

Right-click the port and select **Start**. Now you should see a green symbol indicating that the status has changed to Started.

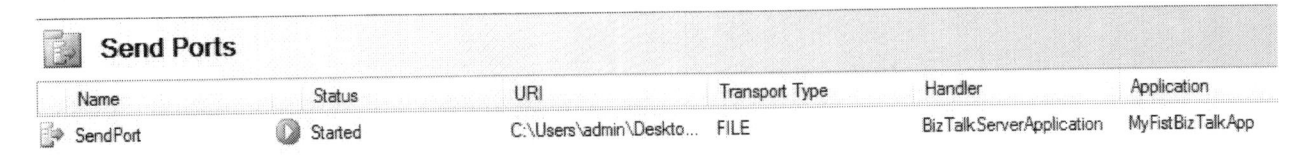

Figure 86: Started port

Configure the Orchestration

This is our last configuration step, and we are simply going to bind our physical ports to the logical ports developed in our orchestration. Double-click your orchestration in the Orchestration folder; you will see the Orchestration Properties window in the tree view on the left of the Administrator. Select the host, choosing the default **BizTalk Server Application**, and for each receive and send port, use the combo box to bind them to the physical ports created previously in this Administrator Console. Once you complete this step, our application configuration is complete, and we are ready to start and test it.

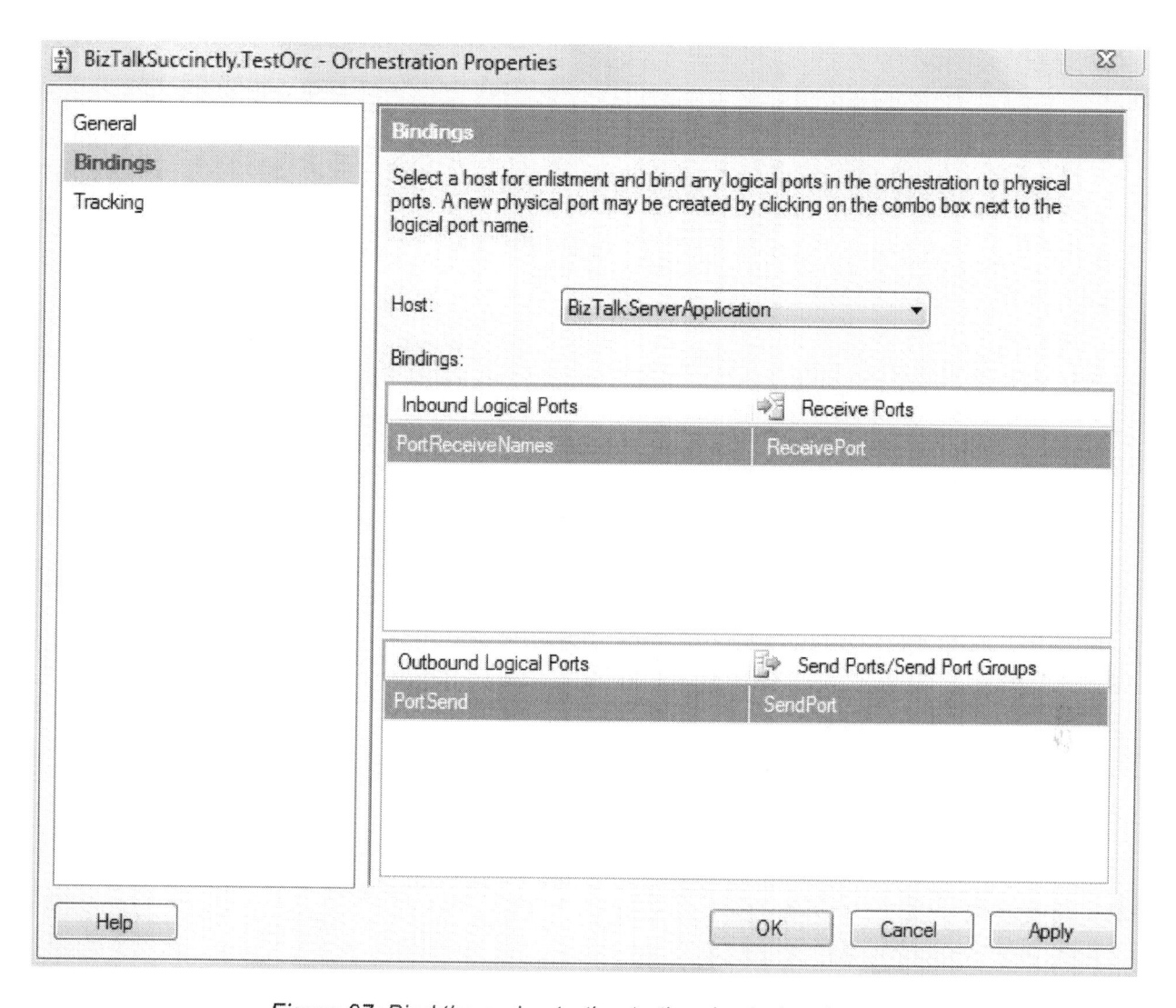

Figure 87: Bind the orchestration to the physical ports

Start the application

The next step is to start the application, which is a very simple step: just right-click **MyFirstBizTalkApp** and select **Start...**. Next, BizTalk will ask if you want to start, and you should select **Start** to confirm.

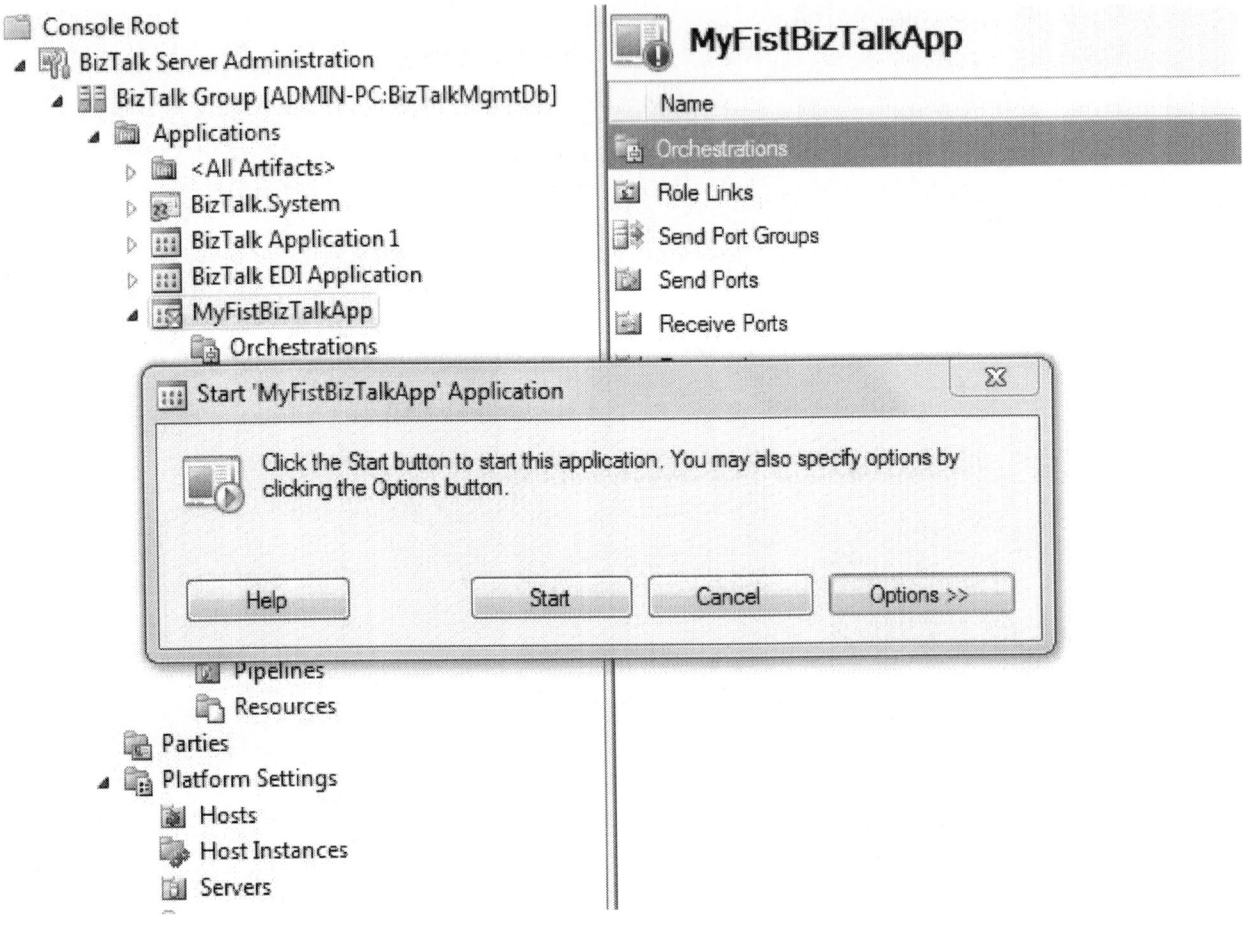

Figure 88: Start the application

Test the application

This is our final step—testing that the application works. To do so, we need to build our XML message; for this example I will use the code shown in Figure 89.

```xml
<?xml version="1.0"?>
<ns0:Root xmlns:ns0="http://BizTalkSuccinctly.OrcSource">
    <PersonName>
        <FisrtName>Rui</FisrtName>
        <MiddleName>Silva</MiddleName>
        <LastName>Machado</LastName>
    </PersonName>
    <PersonName>
        <FisrtName>We</FisrtName>
        <MiddleName>Love</MiddleName>
        <LastName>Syncfusion</LastName>
    </PersonName>
    <PersonName>
        <FisrtName>Toy</FisrtName>
        <MiddleName>Love</MiddleName>
        <LastName>Singer</LastName>
    </PersonName>
    <PersonName>
        <FisrtName>Tony</FisrtName>
        <MiddleName>The Man</MiddleName>
        <LastName>Carreira</LastName>
    </PersonName>
    <PersonName>
        <FisrtName>Agata</FisrtName>
        <MiddleName>Portuguese</MiddleName>
        <LastName>Singer</LastName>
    </PersonName>
</ns0:Root>
```

Figure 89: Input xml

Now let's use it in our receive location. Just go to your **Receive Server** folder and drop the input's XML file. If everything goes well with the configurations, BizTalk will automatically make it disappear.

Figure 90: Drop the input file to the receive location

Once the file disappears, go to your **Send Server** location, which should contain a new message.

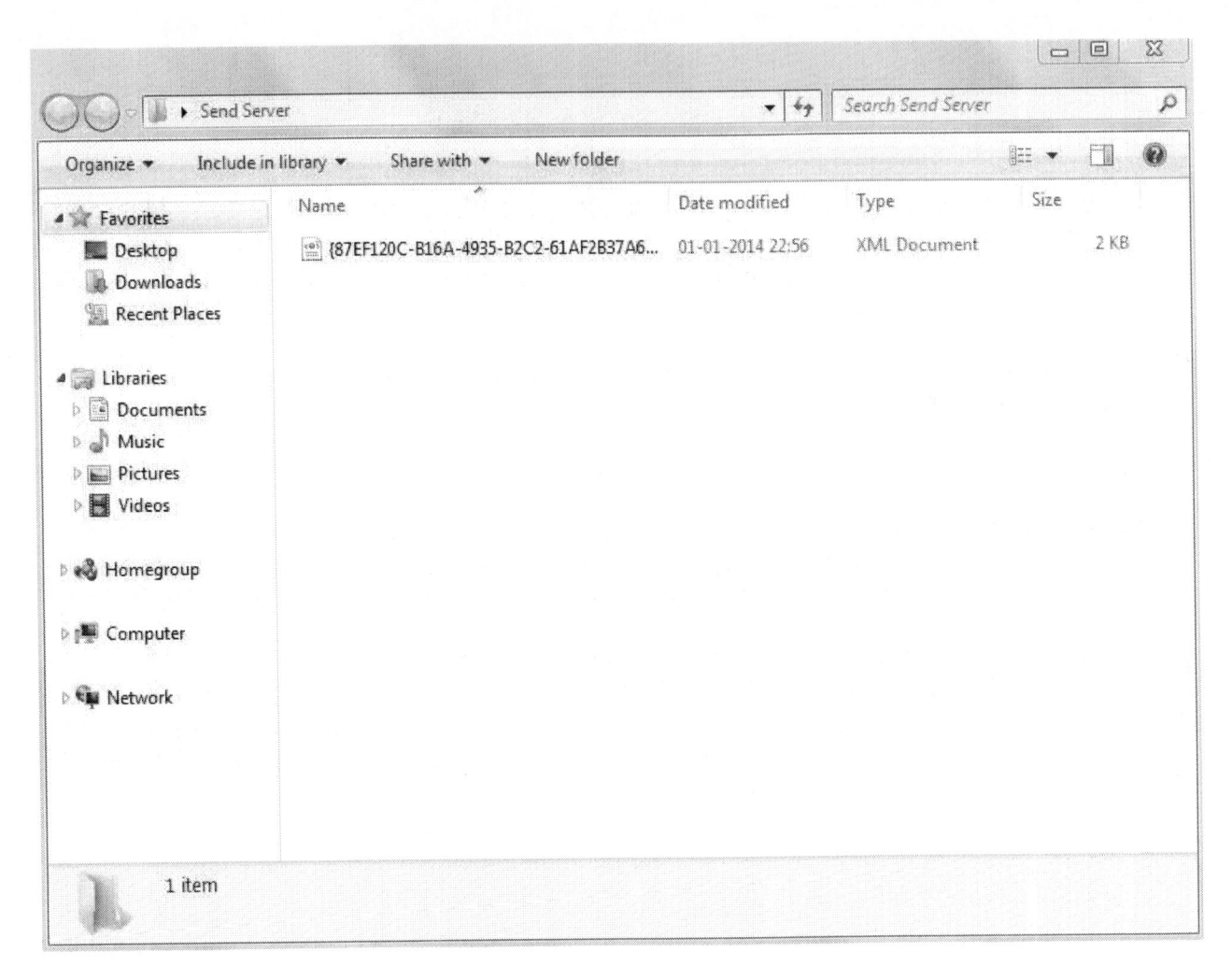

Figure 91: Send Server with new message

If you open this file, you will see that the input message was transformed using our developed map, and the expected result is shown in Figure 92:

```xml
<?xml version="1.0"?>
<ns0:Root xmlns:ns0="http://BizTalkSuccinctly.OrcDestination">
    <Person>
        <FullName>FirstName:Rui|| MiddleName:Silva|| LastName:Machado</FullName>
    </Person>
    <Person>
        <FullName>FirstName:We|| MiddleName:Love|| LastName:Syncfusion</FullName>
    </Person>
    <Person>
        <FullName>FirstName:Toy|| MiddleName:Love|| LastName:Singer</FullName>
    </Person>
    <Person>
        <FullName>FirstName:Tony|| MiddleName:The Man|| LastName:Carreira</FullName>
    </Person>
    <Person>
        <FullName>FirstName:Agata|| MiddleName:Portuguese|| LastName:Singer</FullName>
    </Person>
</ns0:Root>
```

Figure 92: Result message

One Last Note

BizTalk Server is a powerful platform that can be applied to multiple project types. It not only allows you to integrate data, use business rules engines, and monitor your business using its Business Activity Monitoring, it allows you to connect people, systems, and businesses using business processes and workflows. Another nice feature that I haven't talked about in this book is the ability to create Electronic Data Interchange (EDI) projects, which is more than a standard for exchanging documents between business partners.

This book was meant to show you how to start developing with this platform; however, BizTalk has inspired a whole world of professions around it, including developers, database administrators, managers, integration consultants, and much more. There are many resources available to you if you wish to continue your learning.

Although it might seem like a new technology, it has existed since the year 2000, and many people share their knowledge every day on topics related to this platform. Time spent studying it is a valuable investment, and I am pretty sure it will open many business opportunities for you.

My final note goes to BizTalk Server 2013 R2, which brings even more powerful features to this product. One of the biggest features is the ability to connect your applications to Azure services, eliminating the need to have a physical infrastructure to develop some integration solutions, as well as significant improvements in its adapters and execution efficiency. If you feel comfortable with BizTalk Server 2010, you should give this version a try.

Printed in Great Britain
by Amazon.co.uk, Ltd.,
Marston Gate.